CHRISTIANS
IN COMMUNION

Paul Avis

GEOFFREY
CHAPMAN
MOWBRAY

Geoffrey Chapman Mowbray
A Cassell imprint
Villiers House, 41–47 The Strand, London WC2N 5JE, England
© Paul Avis 1990

First published 1990

British Library Cataloguing in Publication Data
Avis, Paul D. L. *1947–*
    Christians in communion.
    1. Christian church. Ecumenical movement
    I. Title
    262.0011
ISBN 0–264–67203–8

Typeset by Area Graphics Ltd, Letchworth, Herts
Printed and bound in Great Britain by
Biddles Ltd, Guildford and King's Lynn

Contents

Preface

If there is one fundamental conviction underlying everything in this book, it is the conviction that the Churches' quest for unity involves *a journey into deeper mutual understanding in the context of unconditional mutual acceptance grounded on our common baptism into the Body of Christ and demanding visible expression in a common eucharist.*

The journey into deeper mutual understanding reveals ever more clearly what Christians of separated traditions have in common — 'one Lord, one faith, one baptism, one God and Father of us all' (Ephesians 4.5f.). But paradoxically, it actually yields pessimistic conclusions about the prospects for the structural reunion of the Churches. However, the context of unconditional mutual acceptance holds great potential for our future coming together in more informal, personal and spontaneous ways. Let me explain this paradox.

The participants in interconfessional dialogue tend to see one another's traditions through spectacles somewhat rose-tinted by the fellowship and affection that has blossomed as they have studied, prayed and relaxed together over the years. But a deeper penetration into the legacy — the trust deeds, as it were — of the great traditions (whether embodied in binding decrees, encrusted with anathemas, of Popes and Councils, as in Roman Catholicism, or in a consensus of theologians undergirded by centuries of worshipping and pastoring, as in Anglicanism and Orthodoxy) reveals the extremely limited scope that great ecclesiological traditions have for manoeuvre. They are prisoners of their past, for good or ill.

Anglicans are currently rediscovering their heritage and drawing resources for the strengthening of identity and for the ecumenical task. The Orthodox see no need to adapt the legacy of the past to the fresh demands of the present. They believe that all should remain 'as it was in the beginning, is now, and ever shall be'. There are many Roman Catholics who would like to see a dynamic development of certain aspects of their tradition and a rapid withering away of other aspects. But the great ideological juggernaut is not so easily turned around.

Since Vatican II, Rome has made a number of gestures of ecumenical goodwill towards the Orthodox, Anglicanism and the

Churches of the Reformation. But not one has in any way detracted from Rome's inflexible insistence on its absolute claims. Rome sees its ecumenical involvement as part of its missionary activity which takes the *ecumene* as its parish. The present Pope speaks boldly of his universal God-given mission. There is no diminution of the papal claim to immediate universal jurisdiction. In practice this has been strengthened during the present pontificate, through the imposition of bishops against local preferences and through the suppression of dissenting theologians. The Pope rules the Church. The teaching of John Paul II stresses the identity of the Church with Christ — and its corollary, the papacy as the expression of Christ's government of his Church. The rest of the hierarchy is reduced to a supporting cast and can only give advice when the Pope requests it. The Pope exercises authority over the Church in all matters of faith and morals, for the Church's own good. Rome is still very much — perhaps more than ever — a hierarchical society claiming the full panoply of divine privileges to legislate for the universal Church (*societas perfecta hierarchica*).

Orthodoxy, Anglicanism and the Reformation Churches are united in resisting the Roman claim to universal jurisdiction, but all — even the Reformers — have consistently refused to rule out a certain primacy of honour and some kind of constitutional presidency for the Bishop of Rome. However, Rome is totally uninterested in any such emasculated role. The Pope does not wish to become a symbol — not even a symbol of universal *koinonia*. To suggest, as the Archbishop of Canterbury did in September 1989 in Rome, that the Pope might like to consider a primacy of love and honour by mutual agreement is, on the face of it, as quixotic as suggesting to Margaret Thatcher, the Iron Lady, that she might sweeten her style in the Cabinet with love and kisses. I prefer to interpret Dr Runcie's initiative as an exercise in straight talking: 'This is the only kind of primacy that Anglicans will ever accept, so why not think about it'.

I really do not believe that unity between Churches that do not even recognize each other's ministries, jurisdictions or dogmas will ever come by negotiation and compromise and I am not suggesting that this is what ecumenical dialogues, such as ARCIC, are engaged in — their vital work is concerned with clearing away obstacles, uncovering common ground and clarifying remaining differences. Unity will only come spontaneously, from the heart of the people of God, from the fullness of the Body of Christ.

At the time of writing, the peoples of Eastern Europe are taking to the streets; radical reforms are in hand, barriers between peoples are being literally broken down. Humanity is on the move and enjoying its first taste of freedom. Totalitarian structures — hierarchical ruling bodies, unrepresentative assemblies, presidencies for life — are tumbling. The will of the people is prevailing, at least for the time being. They will not be for ever separated from their kith and kin on the far side of a man-made wall. The reasons are not merely ideological but primarily economic — people are hungry, poor and deprived. Centralized state socialism cannot satisfy their hunger. At this rate, the only relic of centralized authoritarianism in Europe will be the Vatican!

Similarly in the Church: Christians are spontaneously discovering that they are already one in Christ through their common baptism into his Body the Church. They are recovering the truth of the baptismal basis of communion and entering into the *koinonia*, the shared participation in Christ through the Holy Spirit. They are beginning to see that baptism is the only necessary condition for Holy Communion. Their great desire is to be in communion with those who are already in communion with our Lord through the means of grace and who long to be in communion with them. They will not be held back much longer by a paternalistic and authoritarian hierarchy that claims to withhold that privilege for their own good. But their motivation is not primarily theological: it is elemental — they hunger for communion with their fellow Christians. Roman Catholics are increasingly following their convictions in this matter. Thank God for the teaching that obedience to conscience comes before obedience to Church law!

The baptismal basis of communion has been called an ecumenical time-bomb: I would like to help it go off!

Theologians of other traditions have already begun to explore the concept of communion (*koinonia*) — notably John Zizioulas for the Orthodox in his *Being as Communion* and J.-M. R. Tillard for Roman Catholicism in his *Église d'Églises* (unfortunately I was not able to study these until a late stage in my own work — no copy of Tillard's book was available for inter-library loan in this country until November 1989!). But I think that *Christians in Communion* can fairly claim to be the first substantial *Anglican* theology of *koinonia* and also the first *fully ecumenical* treatment of its theme, in the sense that it is not content merely to draw on the resources of Anglican ecclesiology — ample and undervalued though they are — but also attempts to wrestle with the Roman Catholic, Orthodox and Reformation traditions in order to establish its conclusions on as broad a base as possible.

This book is a sequel to two earlier studies. At the conclusion of my *Ecumenical Theology* (1986) I called for a radical ecclesiology that would penetrate to the deep foundation of the Christian Church, to the heart of the Church's life as the Body of Christ. I suggested that the aim of ecumenical theology was to identify and help to liberate and mobilize the inner dynamic of Christian existence in the Church. This is the task that I have tried to tackle in the present book by exploring the New Testament concept of *koinonia*, its foundation in baptism, and its ecumenical implications. If our baptismal incorporation into the Body of Christ is enough to make us Christians, enough to make us members of a Christian Church, enough to make us communicants within that Church, is it not enough to justify intercommunion?

In *Anglicanism and the Christian Church* (1989) I attempted a critical analysis of the tradition of Anglican ecclesiology, distinguishing three models, types or paradigms: the Erastian paradigm (the unity of Church and State in the one Christian commonwealth), the apostolic paradigm (which vested everything in the episcopal succession) and the baptismal paradigm. I showed that the first two were no longer living options for Anglicans, while the third, the baptismal paradigm, was firmly grounded in the consensus of Anglican theologians, from Hooker onwards, and in the teaching of the Lambeth Conferences. The baptismal paradigm is the authentic model for Anglicanism: it recognizes Christians as Christians and Churches as Churches on the basis of their baptism.

Anglicanism has begun to implement this principle in its ecumenical policy, by demolishing the barriers to eucharistic hospitality. All Christians who are communicants in their own Churches are welcome to receive Holy Communion at Anglican altars. Conversely, Anglicans should be assured that an authentic Anglican understanding of the Church would by all means encourage them to accept the eucharistic hospitality of other Churches — even non-episcopal ones (cf. the interim eucharistic sharing agreement between Anglicans and Lutherans in the United States). Where there is baptism there is the Body of Christ, and where there is the Body of Christ who are we to say that there is no sacrament of the Body of Christ?

Christians in Communion attempts to explore the wider ecumenical foundations and implications of the baptismal paradigm of Christian ecclesiology. My hope is that it may play its part in providing resources for the development of the theology of *koinonia* in an ecumenical context and within the Anglican Communion. But above all my prayer is that it may strengthen our sense of the overriding moral imperative that we *ought* to be in communion with our fellow Christians — and so lead to action — whether official or unofficial I do not much care.

Some of the material in this book has been given as lectures on various occasions: to Anglican, Methodist, and Roman Catholic ordinands at The Queen's College, Birmingham; to the 1989 Clergy School at St Michael's College, Llandaff; at St Stephen's House, Oxford; as in-service training for clergy of the dioceses of Exeter and Bath and Wells; and at the Hooker Group, Exeter Cathedral.

For encouragement, advice and practical assistance I am grateful to

Christopher Hill, Alister McGrath, Paul McPartlan, Charles Napier, Nicholas Sagovsky, Rowan Williams and Tom Wright. However, none of these should be implicated in the views expressed in this book which are my own. My thanks also go to Ruth McCurry of Cassell (Mowbray/Geoffrey Chapman) for her editorial support and efficiency, and to my typist Gillian Piper for her dedication and skill beyond the call of duty.

I have incorporated some material from my articles: 'Luther's theology of the Church' (*Churchman*), 'The shaking of the Seven Hills' (*Scottish Journal of Theology*), and 'Reflections on ARCIC II' (*Theology*).

Paul Avis
Stoke Canon Vicarage,
Exeter
November 1989

Abbreviations

ARCIC   Anglican–Roman Catholic International Commission

BEM   *Baptism, Eucharist and Ministry*, the Lima Report of the WCC Faith and Order Commission (Geneva, 1982)

BNTC   *Black's New Testament Commentary*, edited by H. Chadwick (London)

CF   *The Christian Faith in the Doctrinal Documents of the Catholic Church*, ed. J. Neuner and J. Dupuis (London, 1983)

DS   H. Denzinger and A. Schönmetzer (eds) *Enchiridion Symbolorum* (Freiburg im Breisgau, 1963)

EP   R. Hooker, *Of the Laws of Ecclesiastical Polity*, ed. J. Keble (Oxford, 1845)

FR   *Final Report* of ARCIC I (London, 1982)

LACT   Library of Anglo-Catholic Theology

L88   *The Truth Shall Make You Free: The Lambeth Conference 1988* (London, 1988)

LW   *Luther's Works* (St Louis and Philadelphia, 1955–)

NCBC   *New Century Bible Commentary*, ed. R. L. Clements and M. Black (London and Grand Rapids)

NEB   New English Bible

PS   Parker Society edition of the English Reformers

RSV   Revised Standard Version

SC   *Salvation and the Church*, ARCIC II (London, 1987)

SCDF   Sacred Congregation for the Doctrine of the Faith

ST   St Thomas Aquinas, *Summa Theologiae*, Blackfriars edn

T&T   J. Calvin, *Tracts and Treatises* (Grand Rapids, 1958)

TDNT   *Theological Dictionary of the New Testament* (Grand Rapids, 1964–75)

V2   *The Documents of Vatican II*, ed. W. M. Abbott (London, 1966)

WA   M. Luther, *D. Martin Luthers Werke*, Weimarer Ausgabe (Weimar, 1883–)

WCC   World Council of Churches

1

Communion: a challenge to the Christian Churches

The last decade of the second millennium of Christianity is a good time to adjust our perspective on the unity of the Christian Church. The millennium began with the separation, amid mutual anathemas, of East and West. Its midpoint was marked by the further division between the ancient patriarchate of the West, the see of Rome, and the national churches of the Protestant Reformation who, like the East, resisted its jurisdiction. But the end of the second millennium coincides with the close of a remarkable ecumenical century in which the historic Christian traditions, after seeming to move apart for so long, have begun to gravitate towards each other again. This dual perspective invites an assessment of the successes and failures of the ecumenical enterprise. That assessment should be conducted with candid realism. How does the profit and loss account look after a century of gradual Christian convergence?

On the one hand great strides have been made in the ecumenical quest — that ongoing journey of deeper understanding in the context of unconditional mutual acceptance. If ecumenical progress were measured in goodwill, in love, affection and esteem, in what we have learnt from one another's traditions, and in informal patterns of fellowship and co-operation, then the ecumenical venture must be judged a resounding success. Remarkable theological agreements on many of the issues that have divided the Church in the past — for example, sacraments, ministry, justification — have been concluded between Roman Catholics and Lutherans, Roman Catholics and Anglicans, Anglicans and Lutherans, Anglicans and Reformed. These have prepared the ground for closer communion.

But the breakthrough has not come. Early hopes have been disappointed. The Christian Churches are still separated and the historic traditions largely remain out of communion with each other. While Christians still cannot say, 'We are one body for we all partake of the one bread' (1 Corinthians 10.17), the ecumenical movement is failing. While Rome and the Orthodox remain ambivalent about the ecclesial status of other episcopal churches and Anglicans are paralysed in their approach to non-episcopal churches, ecumenical

1

theology has not probed deep enough. Theological agreed statements perform the indispensable function of clearing away obstacles to communion, but before communion can become a reality, we need a deeper exploration of the meaning and grounds of communion itself.

The new ecumenical realism invites a fresh approach to Christian unity

The visit of the Archbishop of Canterbury, Dr Robert Runcie, to Rome in September 1989 injected a healthy dose of realism into our inveterate romanticizing about Christian unity. Ecumenism is sustained by hope but vitiated by illusion. Under the pontificate of John Paul II, Rome has certainly not raised false hopes about the prospects of a major breakthrough. It has shunned diplomatic ambiguities and has not been afraid of tough talking. Cardinal Ratzinger, responding to the *Final Report* of the first Anglican–Roman Catholic International Commission (ARCIC I), demanded a clearer and more specific Anglican theological profile to engage with. Cardinal Willebrands, then head of the Pontifical Council for the Promotion of Christian Unity, addressing the Assembly of the Lutheran World Federation in Budapest in 1984, insisted that ecumenical dialogue must not blur historic confessional identity. The diversities of the Christian tradition should be reconciled, not glossed over. Future unity between churches that had lost their sense of communal identity, loyalty and self-respect, would be meaningless. Willebrands therefore called for a 'reconfessionalization' of the ecumenical movement. In his reply to the Archbishop of Canterbury's letter following the Lambeth Conference of Anglican bishops worldwide in 1988, the Pope bluntly insisted that the ordination of women in the Anglican Communion would 'effectively block the path to the mutual recognition of ministries'.

During his meeting with the Archbishop of Canterbury, Dr Robert Runcie, in September 1989, Pope John Paul II reaffirmed the 'universal primacy . . . in action and initiative' of the successor of Peter, and reiterated that the ordination of women to the priesthood and episcopate in the Anglican Communion had 'seriously aggravated the differences between us'. The Pope insisted that unity could only come about on the basis of 'the integrity of the apostolic faith', which could only be guaranteed by the magisterium, that is, by the teaching office of the bishops in communion with the Pope acting corporately. The Pope clearly did not see the Anglican bishops in communion with the Archbishop of Canterbury as having a part to play in preserving the apostolic faith.

The Archbishop was equally blunt. 'Realism and honesty' compelled him to acknowledge that the ordination of women in the Anglican Communion seemed to the Roman Catholic Church to have exceeded the bounds of legitimate diversity. The Archbishop went on boldly to imply that the only sort of papal primacy that might be acceptable to Anglicans would be a primacy of love for the sake of unity and mission — primacy that would respect the integrity of local churches. For the benefit of his Protestant critics, the Archbishop might have added that this was precisely the sort of primacy for which the sixteenth-century Reformers and their successors were often careful to leave the door open.

The common declaration by the Pope and the Archbishop at the conclusion of their meeting referred again to the question of the admission of women to holy orders. 'These differences in faith', it stated, 'reflect important ecclesiological differences.' They urged the Anglican–Roman Catholic International Commission and all others working in the ecumenical field 'not to minimize these differences'.

In this bracing climate of cordial realism, it has become clear once again that historic Christian traditions have little room for manoeuvre. They retain their essential character through the centuries. Change is extremely slow and can only come about by a gradual evolution that preserves continuity with the past. Rome is still a hierarchical society complete in itself (*societas perfecta*), claiming plenitude of divine authority to legislate in belief and practice for the whole Church. Bellarmine's Counter-Reformation definition still stands:

> The one and true Church is the community of men brought together by the profession of the same Christian faith and conjoined in the communion of the same sacraments, under the government of legitimate pastors and especially the one Vicar of Christ on earth, the Roman pontiff. (Dulles, p. 14)

The magisterium that ruled in 1896 that Anglican orders were 'absolutely null and utterly void' is unlikely to reverse that decision because of a shift in ecumenical sentiment (cf. Hughes).

On the other hand, it is clear that the Anglican Communion remains a family of Churches grounded firmly in the tradition of reformed catholicism. It continues to hold dear the principle of provincial autonomy and dispersed authority against any centralizing pretentions. As a tradition that welcomed the new learning and insights of the humanist Renaissance in the sixteenth century, Anglicanism can hardly refuse to give hospitality to the insights of the twentieth-century social sciences that have exposed the oppressive patriarchal character of traditional society as far as women are concerned. Anglicanism will not be restrained from acting on the moral imperative deriving from that insight because that incorrigibly patriarchal institution, the Roman hierarchy, does not accept it!

Progress in unity will not be attained by pretending that the historic Christian traditions — Rome, the Orthodox, the Reformation

Churches, Anglicanism — are other than they are. This sounds, I know, like a counsel of despair. So where is hope to be found? The way forward, I believe, is to dig deeper for a ground of unity that transcends our ideological and historical divergencies. That ground is our common incorporation into the Body of Christ by baptism — and its corollary that baptism is a sufficient basis for admission to Communion. When we are in communion with one another in the one way that has clear dominical authority, our historical differences may well appear in a different light. Biological change comes about in response to urgent stimuli emerging from the environment of an organism. Inject a new element into the environment and you quicken radical change.

The professed aim of the ecumenical adventure is structural unity. For example, the goal of ARCIC is 'the restoration of full ecclesial communion' between the Roman and the Anglican Churches. When unpacking this gleaming phrase, we would be well advised not to be misled by the word 'restoration' into overlooking the saga of unedifying conflicts, rivalries, resentments and power struggles that were the mark of relations between the English Church and Rome *before* the Reformation. Full structural unity is bound to be a dominantly political achievement. Its structures will be able to claim little basis in the New Testament. I believe that there is a prior imperative — above the political stands the mystical — and that is to explore more profoundly the central New Testament conception of communion (*koinonia*) and the radical consequences that it has for our emerging ecumenical theology. I confess I remain profoundly unimpressed by the prospect of interlocking structures of jurisdiction and decision-making. I still prefer to measure progress in these matters by the growth of charity, mutual unconditional acceptance (which psychotherapy has taught us is the precondition of all truly therapeutic relationships), and above all, by the nearer prospect of kneeling together to receive the one bread and to drink from the one cup.

In the remaining sections of this chapter I shall try to show that the question of intercommunion has acquired a new urgency for Roman Catholics and Anglicans in particular and then go on to ask whether recent broader ecumenical dialogue can point us the way forward in this matter of communion.

For Roman Catholics, the quest for the reunion of the churches has called forth a new commitment in which the question of communion presents itself for decision

For some years the ecumenical movement seems to have been marking time while the partners waited to see whether the Roman Catholic

Church would commit itself to the reunion of the Church on the basis of unreserved mutual acceptance. Its approach to ecumenism has always been one of extreme caution. During the First World War, Pope Benedict XV declined invitations on two occasions to send Roman Catholic representatives to Faith and Order conferences. The Holy Office inhibited Roman Catholics from participating in Life and Work at Stockholm in 1925 and Faith and Order at Lausanne two years later. In 1928 Pius XI condemned the ecumenical movement in the encyclical *Mortalium animos*. When the World Council of Churches was formed after the Second World War, the Holy Office refused to allow Roman Catholics to participate in the first assembly in 1948 at Amsterdam or the second in 1954 at Evanston.

A more positive approach was first intimated in the papal instruction *Ecclesia Catholica* in 1949, and in 1952 J. Willebrands set up the unofficial 'International Catholic Conference for Ecumenical Questions', the precursor of John XXIII's Secretariat for Promoting Christian Unity. In 1961 Rome had observers at the WCC assembly in New Delhi, but the watershed was the Decree on Ecumenism *Unitatis Redintegratio* of the Second Vatican Council in 1964. In 1968 Roman Catholic theologians officially participated in the Faith and Order Commission of the World Council of Churches for the first time. But unlike the Orthodox, Rome has never joined the WCC. Thus a specific, tangible commitment was still lacking. That could only be meaningfully given at the local, regional level.

As far as England is concerned the Roman Catholic leadership has now given that long-awaited signal and the new ecumenical situation has been created. The catalyst and symbol of this is the Swanwick Declaration of 4 September 1987, to which representatives of 32 Churches, including the Roman Catholic Church, subscribed. The Declaration was entitled 'Not Strangers but Pilgrims'. The signatories rejoiced that they were pilgrims together on the path to unity and strangers no longer. They confessed that they were ready to commit themselves to one another under God. The heart of the declaration urged that 'as a matter of policy at all levels and in all places, our churches must now move from co-operation to clear commitment'. They pledged themselves never to let go of the hope and vision that had become theirs, and professed themselves ready to take risks to bring the vision to realization.

One of those risks had already been taken by Cardinal Basil Hume in an address the day before the Declaration was approved. He pledged the Catholic Church in England to move forward in taking the decisive step from co-operation to commitment, taking his stand not only on the gospel imperative (I assume he was alluding to John 17) but on the mandate provided by the Second Vatican Council. This

5

commitment was to seek for full communion, visible and organic. Cardinal Hume explained what he had in mind in these words (and I am sure that he chose his words with the utmost care):

> By full communion I mean that 'koinonia', that fellowship, that oneness in the Body of Christ, of which the essential elements were already outlined in the Acts of the Apostles, ' . . . be true to the teaching of the Apostles, the breaking of bread, to fellowship and to prayer'.

Cardinal Hume acknowledged that local initiative was the key to implementing this new commitment: there can be 'no authentic evolution of Church unity which does not take place at the local level'. He added significantly: 'we are deeply related to each other in Christ through baptism'.

Perhaps we could be forgiven for wondering whether Cardinal Hume had the authority to make this commitment on the part of the Catholic Church in England. Some at the time — only half in jest — asked whether he was expecting a phone call from the Vatican! The conference came to an emotional end: the Archbishops of Canterbury and Westminster — unable to communicate each other — gave each other their blessing at the altar as one blesses an unconfirmed child. Whether the call from the Vatican ever came I do not know, but we are waiting with eager expectation to see what the payoff will be in terms of Roman Catholic policy regarding local ecumenical initiatives. How will the Swanwick Declaration change the situation in practice?

Cardinal Hume alluded to the grounds of our *koinonia* in our common baptism into Christ, and to the local fruition of this in 'the breaking of bread'. The baptismal basis of Christian communion is an ecumenical time-bomb. When it goes off — when the extent of our *koinonia* as Christians through baptism into the Body of Christ really comes home to us — the question it will leave behind — like a yawning crater in our path — is the question of *intercommunion*.

The 1988 Lambeth Conference, anticipating the imminent election of a woman to the episcopate, put the issue of communion at the top of the agenda for Anglicans

The term 'the Anglican Communion' begins to appear in the mid-nineteenth century (1851 to be precise) to refer to the provinces of the Anglican family that are linked in fellowship through being in communion with each other and with the Archbishop of Canterbury. But only recently have Anglicans been compelled to ask some searching questions about the grounds and nature of the communion they enjoy — its biblical, historical and theological basis. These questions have arisen in two ways. First, they have been generated by the demands of *ecumenical dialogue* when Anglican participants have

6

to research and present a position and are compelled to ask, 'What do we believe? What does our tradition teach? What does unite the diversity of views within our communion?' It must be admitted that Anglicans are not yet very good at getting the right answers to these questions! Second, such questions have also been forced upon Anglicans by the threat to the *cohesion of Anglicanism* now posed by the fact that some provinces of the Anglican Communion have ordained women priests and begun to consecrate women bishops. It is this latter issue, rather than the demands of ecumenism, that has concentrated the minds of the Anglican bishops.

In 1988 Lambeth Conference put the question of communion near the top of the agenda for Anglicans. The Archbishop of Canterbury reminded the gathered bishops that they represented 'not an empire, nor a federation, nor a jurisdiction, not yet the whole Church, but a communion, a fellowship based on our gathering at the Lord's Table'. One of the section reports, that on 'Dogmatic and Pastoral Concerns', takes up the theme:

> The Anglican Communion consists of a family of Churches which say of themselves that they are in communion with each other. At a time when there is debate and disagreement in the family, it is essential to set all consideration of what it might mean to be Anglican in the wider context of the familiar and ancient (indeed biblical) word 'communion'. The fundamental theological question about the identity of Anglicanism is what it means for a Christian to be in communion. (L88, p. 105)

Resolution 18 of the Lambeth Conference, 'The Anglican Communion: Identity and Authority', committed the Anglican churches to a deeper exploration of 'the meaning and nature of communion' — adding with gay abandon that this was to be pursued 'with particular reference to the doctrine of the Trinity, the unity and order of the Church and the unity and community of humanity' (L88, p. 216). That should keep Anglican theologians out of mischief for a while! The Ecumenical Relations section indicated the nature of the connection between the communion of Christians and the life of the Holy Trinity. 'Our unity with one another . . . is grounded in the life of unity and communion of the Godhead. The eternal, mutual, self-giving and receiving love of the three persons of the Trinity' revealed in our Lord's high priestly prayer in John 17, 'is the source and ground of our communion, of our fellowship with God and with one another' (L88, p. 130).

Referring to the collect for All Saints' Day, which speaks of the Church as 'knit together . . . in one communion and fellowship, in the mystical body of . . . Christ', the Conference asked, 'What *is* that communion?' It answered in terms of the believer's baptismal union with Christ — 'the redemptive gift of incorporation into Christ, into our crucified, risen and ascended Lord'. But this union has a horizontal as well as a vertical dimension: 'Communion with Christ also means communion with all those who belong to Christ. Through the response of faith and baptism, Christians enter a living Body, the Church, of persons committed to relationship with each other.' This communion comes to fulfilment in the eucharist, the sacrament of the renewal and unity of all humanity and all creation in God. But here the Lambeth fathers were brought up sharply against the fact of disunity, the absence of eucharistic fellowship. They acknowledged:

> We are brought by the promise of eucharistic fellowship into a relationship of longing and desire with those Christians with whom we do not yet fully enjoy institutional communion, because of prohibitions contained in canon law or imposed by conscience. Here we confront a paradox, in that by mutually recognised baptism we share in a basic bond of incorporation into Christ, a transition and conversion of such momentous importance as to over-shadow all our other divisions.

Quoting the Lima statement (*BEM*), the bishops of the Anglican Communion took up the challenge to overcome division and visibly manifest the fellowship we have with our fellow Christians on the basis of our one baptism into Christ (L88, pp. 105–7).

Arising from the Lambeth Conference, the Anglican Consultative Council (the standing committee of the Anglican Communion) will initiate a study — probably through the Inter-Anglican Theological and Doctrinal Commission — of the structures of Anglicanism as a communion (L88, pp. 5, 293ff.). These structures include *conciliarity* — consultations of primates; *collegiality* — the corporate authority and collective responsibility of the bishops; and *primacy* — the role of the Archbishop of Canterbury. However, it seems an essential prerequisite of this programme that the Anglican Communion should also at last inaugurate a study of the Anglican doctrine of the Church and formulate an outline Anglican ecclesiology. Such a study could lead to the preparation of a substantial document that could hopefully receive some sort of official status in due course — perhaps provisionally from the primates, who could commend it for discussion throughout the Communion, and then ultimately from the next Lambeth Conference.

A formulation of Anglican ecclesiology is urgently needed. Anglican representatives on some recent ecumenical commissions have given every impression of making up Anglican ecclesiology as they go along — for example, flirting with notions of inerrancy or infallibility (under certain technically specifiable conditions) and with claims of a universal primacy by divine right (in the guise of divine permission sanctioned by the providential pattern of history). I have challenged these aberrations in my *Ecumenical Theology*. As Stephen Sykes has insisted, there *is* an Anglican doctrine of the Church (Sykes in Wright (ed.) and Draper (ed.)). I would wish to add, however, that this distinctively Anglican conception of the Church needs to be disentangled from various historical frameworks or paradigms. It needs to be distinguished, first, from what I have designated the 'Erastian paradigm' of a Church governed by the 'godly prince' where Anglicanism was the state monopoly religion, citizenship in the national commonwealth and membership in the Anglican Church were synonymous, and participation in the sacramental ministrations of the Church was compulsory. Second, the authentic Anglican concept of the Church needs to be distinguished from the 'apostolic paradigm' — the High Church and Tractarian reaction to Erastianism, when all the ecclesiological eggs were forced into the basket of apostolic succession. As the cases of Newman and Manning showed, an apostolicity so conceived — the illusory apostolicity of tactile transmission of sacramental grace without which salvation was not assured — was unconvincing without that other credal note of the Church, catholicity. However, in the way that Newman and Manning pursued it — in an empirical, head-counting way, seeking spatio-temporal guarantees for the Church's authority — catholicity could only be assured by the living voice of God on earth — the Pope. I believe that an authentically Anglican interpretation of the catholic and apostolic dimensions of the Church can be rediscovered in the doctrine of baptism — and that, significantly, is also the key to communion. (See further, Avis, *Anglicanism and the Christian Church*.)

These developments within Anglicanism serve to bring the explicit ecclesiological thinking of Anglicans into line with recent trends in ecumenical theology and inter-confessional dialogue. The commission set up by the Archbishop of Canterbury under the chairmanship of Archbishop Robin Eames of Armagh, as a damage-limitation exercise, anticipating the imminent election and consecration of a woman bishop, to examine the ways in which communion between Anglicans might suffer the minimum impairment, was naturally compelled to examine the nature and grounds of the communion enjoyed by Anglicans. It remains to be seen whether the theological cement that the Eames commission has used will prove stronger than the pressures now making for fragmentation. It is my conviction that the understanding of communion being presented in the present book can do much to help contain — if not to actually resolve — the current tensions within the Church of England and the Anglican Communion. But it also has relevance for our ecumenical commitments.

The rediscovery of Anglican ecclesiology, with its exploration of the dynamics and structures of our existing communion, of conciliarity, collegiality and primacy within the Anglican Communion, can help us to make up our minds about the kind of communion, conciliarity, collegiality and primacy that we are seeking in dialogue with our ecumenical partners. For example, it will help us to be clearer in our own minds as to whether we want to see a progressive enlargement, deepening and strengthening of the communion we already enjoy, with its largely moral, personal and social obligations and constraints, or one that is more sharply defined and more closely regulated, with the inevitable canonical and juridical constraints and sanctions.

Ecumenical theology is beginning to take the baptismal basis of communion seriously

In May 1982 Pope John Paul II visited England. He and the Archbishop of Canterbury recalled their one baptism, renewed their baptismal vows and celebrated 'the bond of our common baptism into Christ' (Flannery, p. 187). This act was symbolic of a new ecumenical initiative that is attempting to develop the unitive potential of our common baptism. The ground had been prepared by the work of the first Anglican–Roman Catholic International Commission (ARCIC I).

The commission purported to make communion (*koinonia*) central to its explorations. It asserted: 'Union with God in Christ Jesus through the Spirit is the heart of Christian *koinonia*' (*FR*, p. 6). It went on to point out that '*Koinonia* with one another is entailed by our *koinonia* with God in Christ' (ibid.). It intended that this should be the unifying theme of its work, but it actually confined its explorations to the significance of *koinonia* for three central aspects of the Church's life: the eucharist, the ministry, and primacy in a united Church: 'the eucharist as the effectual sign of *koinonia*, episcope as serving the *koinonia*, and primacy as a visible link and focus of *koinonia*' (ibid.). In practice, the Commission adopted a very specific position on the significance of *koinonia* for these aspects of the Church's life. The eucharist was conceived predominantly as the sign of a communion already achieved rather than as a means to creating that communion. Ministry and oversight (episcope) was basically understood as serving a communion that existed alongside it, rather than as an expression of that communion and created by it. Primacy — that is, the role of the Pope in a united Church — was indeed considered as a visible link and focus of communion, but the significance of communion for the whole nature and exercise of authority in the Church was not explored — although the reports on primacy came out under the rubric of 'Authority'.

More importantly, ARCIC I almost entirely passed over the foundational sacrament of baptism as the ground of *koinonia*. It is indeed implied in the statement: 'In the New Testament it is clear that the community is established by a baptism inseparable from faith and conversion' (*FR*, p. 8). But elsewhere it seems to be implied that the eucharist, rather than baptism, is the ground of *koinonia*: 'By the eucharist all the baptized are brought into communion with the source of *koinonia*' (p. 7). (Whether this sentence: 'into communion with the source of communion' is intentionally tautological is not clear.) Again, at one point the *Final Report* seems to want to base communion on 'the word of God', by which it seems to mean the gospel. 'The *koinonia* is grounded in the word of God preached, believed and obeyed' (p. 8). This seems to be a tentative reaching out towards Reformation, Lutheran theology. However, for the Reformers, the word was never separated from the sacraments. Both together brought the Church into existence, made Christ present, and signalled the fact of a true Church. But it was through baptism that believers were incorporated into Christ and united with one another — and this communion came to expression in the Lord's Supper. The Report is close to this when it says, 'In the New Testament it is clear that the community is established by a baptism inseparable from faith and conversion, that its mission is to proclaim the Gospel of God, and that its common life is sustained by the eucharist' (p. 8). As we shall see in the next chapter, the New Testament is deeply sacramental in its conception of *koinonia*, and it is regrettable that ARCIC I did not develop the baptismal basis of *koinonia*.

Had ARCIC I built on a foundation of agreement on the significance of the sacrament of baptism, I have no doubt that its various statements would have had a rather different slant. For example, a grasp of the baptismal foundation of the ministry of the whole priestly body of the Church would have precluded the profoundly unsatisfactory assertion that the ministry of the ordained 'is not an extension of the common Christian priesthood' but 'belongs to another realm of the gifts of the Spirit' (*FR*, p. 36). This merely parrots one of the least coherent statements of the Second Vatican Council (*Lumen Gentium*, 10) and fails to effect an integration of *koinonia* and ministry. A grasp of the significance of baptism, whereby the believer is invested with Christ's priestly office, would suggest that, since the fullness of priesthood dwells in the whole priestly body of the Church, the ordained ministry must indeed derive its priesthood from this source — i.e. from Christ through his body the Church — for there is no 'other realm' outside the body of Christ to which it might belong (see Chapter 6). Second, a firm foundation for *koinonia* in the sacrament of holy baptism would hardly have permitted the commission to formulate statements on authority in the Church that either omitted or glossed over the role of the laity in the government of the Church. This omission again leads one to question whether all the Anglican representatives on ARCIC I were really in touch with the sources and roots of their own tradition — for if there is one point that belongs firmly to the consensus of Anglican theology, it is the rights and role of the laity (cf. Avis, *Anglicanism and the Christian Church*, pp. 60ff., 287ff.).

The current series of Anglican–Roman Catholic conversations (ARCIC II) appear to be taking the baptismal basis of *koinonia* more seriously than their predecessor. The ARCIC II document on justification, *Salvation and the Church* (1986), finely states: 'Baptism is the unrepeatable sacrament of justification and incorporation into Christ' (p. 18). At the time of writing, the Commission is putting the finishing touches to a document devoted entirely to the theme of *koinonia*. It sees this as the key to resolving the impasse on the question of Anglican orders in general and the Anglican orders of women priests in particular. Whether in this report the Commission will at last go right back to first principles and develop a doctrine of the foundational sacrament of the Christian Church — holy baptism — remains to be seen. But I am convinced that it is only by so doing that they will actually achieve their purpose.

In contrast to ARCIC I, the Lima statement of the Faith and Order Commission of the World Council of Churches, *Baptism, Eucharist and Ministry* (*BEM*, 1982), lays a sure foundation in the doctrine of baptism before proceeding to the doctrines of the eucharist and the ministry. 'Baptism unites the one baptized with Christ and with his people', it affirms. 'Through baptism, Christians are brought into union with Christ, with each other and with the Church of every time and place.' The Lima statement draws attention to the implications of our common baptism for the unity of the Church, citing as did Richard Hooker at the end of the sixteenth century, Ephesians 4.4–6: 'one Lord, one faith, one baptism', and drawing the conclusion: 'our baptism into Christ constitutes a call to the churches to overcome their divisions and visibly manifest their fellowship' (*BEM*, pp. 2–3).

The Anglican–Reformed dialogue *God's Reign and Our Unity* (1984) treats baptism as the foundation of the Church — and therefore also the foundation of its unity. Because it is through our baptism that Christ incorporates us into his life, death and resurrection, baptism is 'in the strictest sense, constitutive of the Church' (p. 33, para. 53). The report draws the conclusion: 'If we are as realistic about baptism as the apostolic writers are, then we are already by our baptism one body, and the continued separation of our two communions is a public denial of what we are already in Christ' (p. 38, para. 61).

The seriousness with which the baptismal basis of communion is being explored in current ecumenical dialogue marks the opening of a new and promising chapter in the story of the Churches' search for unity.

2
Communion
in the New Testament

In the New Testament, communion (*koinonia*) is grounded in baptism and comes to expression in the Lord's Supper

Communion was very real for the first Christians. They had an overwhelming sense of sharing in a reality greater than themselves. There may well be an element of idealization in Luke's portrait of the nascent Christian community in The Acts of the Apostles. But a corporate experience less dynamic than this would hardly have given the Church the momentum that it did indeed possess.

> All who believed were together and had all things in common; and they sold their possessions and goods and distributed them to all, as any had need. And day by day, attending the temple together and breaking bread in their homes, they partook of food with glad and generous hearts, praising God and having favour with all the people. And the Lord added to their number day by day those who were being saved. (Acts 2.44–47)

It is clear that it was through baptism that they entered the community. When those who were 'cut to the heart' by Peter's preaching on the day of Pentecost cried out, 'What shall we do?', Peter replied: 'Repent and be baptized every one of you in the name of Jesus Christ for the forgiveness of your sins; and you shall receive the gift of the Holy Spirit' (Acts 2.37–38). The narrative continues: 'So those who received his word were baptized, and there were added that day about three thousand souls' (2.41). These converts entered immediately and enthusiastically into the fellowship. 'And they devoted themselves to the apostles' teaching and fellowship (*koinonia*), to the breaking of bread and the prayers' (2.42).

Though this 'breaking of bread' is not identical in every respect with the later sacrament of holy communion, the eucharist, it is certainly in continuity with the fellowship meals that Jesus took with his disciples, culminating in the Last Supper, when he invested the meal with the symbolism of his imminent death by associating it with the Passover, the thanksgiving for deliverance from slavery in Egypt, and gave instructions for the disciples to perpetuate his action and so continue the messianic community after his departure.

It was customary for rabbis to break bread with their disciples (the *chaburah*), but Jesus widened the scope of his fellowship to include the outcasts of society, the ritually unclean — tax collectors, prostitutes and other notorious 'sinners' (Luke 5.29–32), for he had come to call 'sinners to repentance'. Those who, according to the Acts of the Apostles, thronged into the infant Church after Pentecost, were indeed penitent sinners: they had undergone a baptism of repentance for the remission of sins and they celebrated their new-found deliverance by breaking bread together with joyful hearts. Their communion was grounded in baptism and came to focus and fulfilment in the fellowship meal that evolved into the central rite of Christianity, the eucharist.

The New Testament writers' concept of communion is expressed in the substantive *koinonia*; in the use of three prepositions: 'in Christ', 'into Christ' and 'with Christ'; and in the images of the body, the bride and the new humanity. Lying behind all these is the fundamental transaction of the incorporation of Christians into Christ through baptism.

The experience and reality of *koinonia*, translated 'communion', or 'fellowship', is fundamental to the corporate life of Christians in the New Testament and is prominent in a number of the traditions. Its primary and only common meaning is participation along with others in something (Campbell). 'Participation' is a translation that does better justice to *koinonia* than 'communion' or 'fellowship', but they do have the merit of reminding us that participation is a shared activity. Paul speaks of the *koinonia* of Christ, the *koinonia* of the Holy Spirit, *koinonia* in the gospel and *koinonia* in Christ's sufferings (1 Corinthians 1.9; 2 Corinthians 13.14; Philippians 1.5; 2.1; 3.10). The Lord's Supper is a communion (*koinonia*) both with the Lord and with his body the Church: 'The cup of blessing which we bless, is it not *koinonia* of the blood of Christ? The bread which we break, is it not *koinonia* of the body of Christ?' (1 Corinthians 10.16). It is a true communion with Christ rather than with the demons behind pagan sacrifices (vv. 20, 21), and a true communion with one another: 'we who are many are one body, for we all partake of the one bread' (v. 17).

The Johannine literature expresses communion in its own distinctive idiom. While the fourth gospel speaks of abiding or dwelling in the Father and the Son and of their love and life abiding in us, the first epistle of John deploys the concept of *koinonia* richly: 'Our *koinonia* is with the Father and with his Son Jesus Christ' (1 John 1.3). The author of 2 Peter speaks of Christians as destined for *koinonia* with the divine nature (2 Peter 1.4).

The expression 'in Christ' (*en Christo*) occurs 165 times in the Pauline writings and occasionally elsewhere. 1 Peter conveys 'peace to all of you that are in Christ', refers to 'your good behaviour in Christ', and speaks of God's 'eternal glory in Christ' (1 Peter 5.14; 3.16; 5.10). Revelation has the expressions 'in Jesus' and 'in the Lord' (Revelation 1.9; 14.13). For Paul himself, the expression 'in Christ' is the key to what the Book of Common Prayer calls the 'mystical union that is betwixt Christ and his Church'. The New English Bible brings out the meaning when it translates 'in Christ' as 'in union with Christ'. As Best has emphasized (p. 8), the preposition *en* has a local flavour. It is a metaphor of locality. 'Christ is the "place" in whom believers are and in whom salvation is.' All the blessings of the Christian existence are given 'in Christ': redemption (Colossians 1.14; Ephesians 1.7), eternal life (Romans 6.23), deliverance from condemnation under the law (Romans 8.1), sanctification (1 Corinthians 1.2), grace (Ephesians 1.6), fullness of life (Colossians 2.10), comfort (Philippians 2.1), and liberty (Galatians 2.14). As we shall see, the fact of baptism is never far from Paul's (or 'Paul's') thoughts in these passages.

However, as Bultmann pointed out, 'in Christ' is not only a soteriological formula, having to do with the salvation of the individual, but an ecclesiological formula too, relating to the reality of the Church (1, p. 33). Whole churches, and the saints corporately conceived are in Christ: Galatians 1.22: 'churches in Christ' (the RSV misses this by translating 'churches of Christ' as does the NEB with its 'Christ's churches'); 1 Thessalonians 1.1: 'the church of the Thessalonians in God the Father and in the Lord Jesus Christ' (cf. 2.14). The saints are conceived as a unity and it is this unity that is just as much in Christ as is the individual believer (Best, p. 25). Believers are united into a single entity in Christ. As Galatians 3.28 puts it: 'you are all one in Christ Jesus'. Here the context is explicitly that of baptism (v. 27).

Reinforcing Paul's doctrine of unity with Christ, expressed in the preposition *en*, is his use of the expression 'with Christ' (*syn Christo*) to convey the solidarity of Christians, individually and corporately, with Christ through baptism. They are described as living with Christ (Romans 6.8), suffering with Christ (Romans 8.17), crucified with Christ (Romans 6.6; Galatians 2.20), dying with Christ (Romans 6.8), buried with Christ (Romans 6.4; Colossians 2.12), made alive with Christ (Colossians 2.13; Ephesians 2.5), raised with Christ (Colossians 2.12; 3.1; Ephesians 2.6), glorified with Christ (Romans 8.17) and reigning in heavenly places with Christ (2 Timothy 2.12; Ephesians 2.16). The formula 'with Christ' refers to the origin of the Christian life, through the solidarity of Christians with Christ in the drama of

16

redemption — a solidarity that is realized sacramentally in baptism — while the 'in Christ' formula describes that life as a continuing state enjoyed from day to day (cf. Best, p. 62).

The third preposition that conveys the New Testament's teaching about the *koinonia* of Christians with God and each other through Christ is 'into' (*eis*) — 'into Christ' (*eis Christo*). It is this preposition that brings out most clearly the baptismal basis of our incorporation into Christ. 'As many of you as were baptized *into* Christ have put on Christ' (Galatians 3.27). 'Do you not know', asks Paul, 'that all of us who have been baptized *into* Christ Jesus were baptized into his death?' (Romans 6.3). This whole passage (Romans 6.3–11) brings together 'into Christ' and 'with Christ' in the setting of baptism. I have emphasized the characteristic Pauline prepositions:

> How can we who died to sin still live in it? Do you not know that all of us who have been baptized *into Christ Jesus* were baptized *into his death*? We were buried therefore *with him* by baptism *into death* so that as Christ was raised from the dead by the glory of the Father, we too might walk in newness of life.
>
> For if we have been united *with him* in a death like his, we shall certainly be united *with him* in a resurrection like his. We know that our old self was crucified *with him* so that the sinful body might be destroyed, and we might no longer be enslaved to sin. For he who has died is freed from sin. But if we have died *with Christ* we believe that we shall also live *with him*. (Romans 6.2–8, emphasis added)

An early parallel is central to the doctrine of the baptismal basis of communion: 'By one Spirit we were all baptized *into* one body' (1 Corinthians 12.13).

The expression 'in the name of' is equivalent to 'into'. In 1 Corinthians Paul asks rhetorically: 'Is Christ divided? . . . Were you baptized in the name of Paul?' (1.13–15). The answer clearly implied is 'No, you were baptized in the name of Christ. He is the ground of your unity. There cannot be divisions when you are one in him.' Matthew employs the same formula to give the dominical mandate for the Church to 'make disciples of all nations, baptizing them in the name of [i.e. into the reality and identity of] the Father and the Son and the Holy Spirit' (Matthew 28.19). In the apostolic preaching, depicted in the Acts of the Apostles, baptism into Christ opened the door to sharing in the gifts and powers of Christ's kingdom: 'Repent and be baptized, every one of you, in the name of Jesus Christ for the forgiveness of your sins, and you shall receive the gift of the Holy Spirit' (Acts 2.38).

To sum up: those who have been baptized *into* Christ, and who have therefore died and been raised *with* Christ, are those who thereafter continue to exist *in* Christ. As we shall see in a moment, this union with Christ is inseparable from communion with his body, the Church.

The equivalents in the Johannine literature to 'in', 'with' and 'into' Christ, are, as we have already noticed, abiding or dwelling 'in me' (John 6.56; 14.20; 15.4–7; 16.33; 17.21), 'in him', 'in us', 'in the Son and in the Father' (1 John 2.6, 24; 5.11, 20). Often the naked preposition 'in' carries the full ontological meaning of communion: 'I am in my Father and you in me and I in you' (John 14.20); 'We are in him who is true' (1 John 5.20). In the so-called high-priestly prayer of John 17, the Lord prays for the unity of those whom the Father has given him out of the world: 'that they may all be one, even as thou Father, art in me, and I in thee, that they also may be in us, that the world may believe' (17.21). The presumably late stratum of the New Testament that we have in the Johannine epistles is consistent with the Pauline witness to the baptismal basis of the communion of Christians with God and with each other. The baptismal profession of faith seems to be implied in 1 John 4.15: 'Whoever *confesses* that Jesus is the Son of God, God abides in him and he in God'. And the baptismal new birth of the believer seems to be implicit in the references to being born of God through believing in the one to whom the water, the Spirit and the blood all bear witness (1 John 5.4–8; cf. John 3.5: 'born of water and the Spirit').

The image of the *body* of Christ — 'the keystone of Paul's theology' (Robinson, *The Body*, p. 9) — identifies the Church with Christ. The familiar Western dualism of body and soul is Hellenistic and alien to biblical anthropology. Thus when Paul urges Christians to present their bodies as a living sacrifice (Romans 12.1), he does not mean that they are to withhold their minds! 'Body' here stands for the whole self (which is not to say that *soma means* 'whole self': cf. Gundry). Similarly, by calling the Church the body of Christ, Paul is implying that the Church is Christ's existence and presence in the world. This becomes explicit in 1 Corinthians 12.12: 'For just as the body is one and has many members, and all the members of the body, though many are one body, *so it is with Christ*'. Michael Ramsey brings out the boldness of this by quoting Calvin: 'He calls Christ the Church' (Ramsey, p. 35; cf. Calvin, p. 264). Compare Romans 12.5: 'We, though many, are *one body in Christ*'.

But if Paul identifies the Church with Christ, he also identifies Christians with the Church. We are familiar with Christian preachers extolling the glory of the Church by invoking the New Testament images of the Church as the body or bride of Christ. This sort of rhetoric can often serve ideological motives — to inculcate conformity and obedience. The implication is often: 'We speak for the Church, the glorious body of Christ, therefore we have Christ's authority to tell you what to believe and how to behave'. But the New Testament's actual usage can be subversive of appeals to universal authority, for it uses the image of the body (and alongside it, the image of the temple) of the local church and of the individual Christian. So these have rights and authority too — as well as duties and obligations.

Paul speaks of the *whole Church* — putting it anachronistically, the catholic Church — only in 1 Corinthians 12.28, 'God has appointed in the Church first apostles . . .'. The transition is made to the whole Church as the body of Christ in Ephesians (whether it is from Paul's own hand is disputed): 'Christ is the head of the church, his body, and is himself its saviour' (5.23). The image is continued in vv. 29–30: 'No man ever hates his own *flesh*, but nourishes and cherishes it, as Christ does the Church, because we are members of his *body*'. This Pauline theology of the whole Church is reinforced by the image of the Church as the temple of the Spirit: 'the household of God, built upon the foundation of the apostles and prophets, Christ Jesus himself being the chief cornerstone, in whom the whole structure is joined together and grows into a holy temple in the Lord; in whom you also are built into it for a dwelling place of God in the Spirit' (Ephesians 2.19–22). 1 Peter 2.4–10 also appears to speak of the whole Church — 'a chosen race, a royal priesthood, a holy nation' — as a temple ('spiritual house') where 'spiritual sacrifices' are offered to God through Christ. The image of indwelling also lies behind Ephesians 1.22 (though the interpretation is disputed): 'the church, which is his body, the fullness of him who fills all in all'.

The *local church*, the congregation with its various spiritual gifts, is also described by Paul as the body of Christ. This is the application of body imagery that undergirds Paul's appeal for mutual consideration and edification in 1 Corinthians: 'Now you are the body of Christ and individually members of it' (12.27). Similarly, the local church at Corinth is the temple of God's Spirit: 'Do you [plural] not know that you are God's temple, and that God's Spirit dwells in you?' (3.16). In what we know as Paul's second epistle to Corinth, he returns to the theme: 'What agreement has the temple of God with idols? For we are the temple of the living God' (2 Corinthians 6.16).

The *individual Christian* is also the body of Christ. Bearing in mind that, for the biblical writers, the body stood for the whole person, we can appreciate the significance of Paul's insistence that 'your bodies are members of Christ' (1 Corinthians 6.15). But to identify the members, limbs or organs of the body of Christ with individual believers is not quite to say that Christians are individually bodies of

Christ. But in this chapter Paul goes further. There are three steps in the argument.

First, 'the body is meant for the Lord and the Lord for the body' (v. 13), so the body of Christians belongs to the Lord and is the object of his care and purpose.

Second, just as whoever 'joins himself to a prostitute becomes one body with her' — the two become one flesh — so 'he who is united to the Lord becomes one spirit with him' (vv. 16–18). Here 'spirit' is not used in antithesis to body, but in antithesis to 'flesh'. Paul means a 'spiritual body' (Robinson, *The Body*, p. 79) — not a body that is immaterial but one that is imperishable (15.44). The contrast between flesh and spirit is familiar in Pauline thought. His gospel concerned God's Son 'who was descended from David according to the *flesh*, and designated Son of God in power according to the *spirit* of holiness by his resurrection from the dead' (Romans 1.3–4). The flesh (*sarx*) is weak, frail, mortal, inglorious and the instrument of sin. The body (*soma*) is the instrument of God's Spirit and purpose. Body and spirit are inseparable: 'there is one body and one spirit' (Ephesians 4.4). The spirit (or Spirit) of Jesus dwells in his body, the Church. So Paul could equally well say: 'He who is joined to the Lord is one body with him'.

Finally, this is supported by the image of the temple: just as the universal Church and the local church are the temples of the Spirit, so too is the individual believer: 'Do you not know that your body is a temple of the Holy Spirit within you, which you have from God?' (1 Corinthians 6.19). It was at baptism that they became the dwelling place of the Spirit: 'By one Spirit we were all baptized into one body . . . and all were made to drink of one Spirit' (1 Corinthians 12.13). The baptismal drama of death and resurrection implies that 'the Spirit of him who raised Jesus from the dead dwells in you' (Romans 8.11). In the light of all we know of the centrality, subtlety and flexibility of Paul's body theology, it is clear that when he exhorts Christians to 'put on the Lord Jesus Christ' (Romans 13.14), it is putting on a body, not putting on a suit of clothes, that he means (Robinson, *The Body*, p. 63; cf. 2 Corinthians 5.1–10).

However, Paul did not invent the concept of the identity of Christians, corporately and individually, with the body of Christ or the image of the temple. They have a firm dominical basis. The false witnesses at the trial of Jesus accused him of claiming that he would destroy the temple made with hands, and in three days build another, not made with hands (Mark 14.58). Even if the reference to three days is secondary, it was certainly believed that Jesus had foretold the destruction of the temple (13.1–2) and its replacement with a spiritual temple. John makes the connection when he says, 'He spoke of the temple of his body' (John 2.21) and it is John who gives the interpretation when Jesus tells the woman of Samaria at Jacob's well: 'the hour is coming when neither on this mountain nor in Jerusalem will you worship the Father . . . the true worshippers will worship the Father in spirit and truth' — through the messiah (4.21, 26).

Paul would presumably not have known John's gospel, so what was it in the traditions he had received that led him to elaborate his immensely subtle theology of the body of Christ? Surely we have the answer (though Best does not agree: p. 91) in the narrative that Paul 'received of the Lord' concerning the words and acts of Jesus at the Last Supper: 'that the Lord Jesus on the night when he was betrayed, took bread, and when he had given thanks, he broke it and said, "This is my body which is for you. Do this in remembrance of me" ' (1 Corinthians 11.23–24). Here there is an implied transition from receiving to becoming, from eating to sharing, from 'This is my body' to 'You are my body'. This identification of Christ and the Church was no doubt first suggested to Paul/Saul at his encounter with the risen Christ on the Damascus road. 'Who are you, Lord?' he asked. 'I am Jesus whom you are persecuting', came the reply. In persecuting the Church, Saul was injuring Christ himself. This interpretation goes back at least as far as Augustine and is ratified by a consensus of modern scholars (Richardson, p. 251n; Robinson, *The Body*, p. 58; Mersch, p. 104; Ramsey, p. 37).

So, in tracing the body theology through Paul's writings, we are never far from the import of the Last Supper and its perpetuation in the eucharist. Paul can use 'body' with several layers of intentional ambiguity. In his admonition to the Corinthians for their unseemly behaviour at the Lord's supper, Paul warns them of the danger of 'not discerning the body' (1 Corinthians 11.27–29). Does this mean not treating the *sacrament* with proper respect, or not behaving in a manner appropriate to the *Church* as the body of Christ, or not showing brotherly care and love to the humbler *members*, but rather humiliating them (as v. 11 would suggest)? The last interpretation could draw support from Matthew 25.31–46: 'As you did it (not) to one of the least of these (my brethren), you did it (not) to me'. Thus Paul's use of body has moved through several stages: from the sacramental to the ecclesiological to the Christological. As Minnear comments, 'discerning the body' implies 'such an interdependence of the Crucified with his own that a denial of *koinonia* with them is in fact a denial of *koinonia* with him' (p. 188).

When he speaks of the Church as Christ's body, Paul is not conscious of elaborating a metaphor. Robinson comments: 'It is almost impossible to exaggerate the materialism and crudity of Paul's doctrine of the church as literally now the resurrection *body* of Christ . . . . The body that he has in mind is as concrete and as singular as the body of the Incarnation. His underlying conception is not of a suprapersonal collective, but of a specific personal organism' (*The Body*, p. 51; but cf. Gundry, ch. 17). Mascall similarly insists that 'the description of the church as the body of Christ is to be taken ontologically and realistically' (p. 112). Thornton gets to the heart of Paul's ecclesiology when he writes: 'We are members of that body which was nailed to the cross, laid in the tomb and raised to life on the third day' (p. 298). Bonhoeffer could sum up the thesis of his youthful work *Sanctorum Communio* as 'Christ exists as the Church'. But the body image in Paul is not only a way of exalting the Church. It also identifies every Christian with the body of Christ. The consequences of this for ecumenical theology are not far to seek.

The image of the Church as the *bride* of Christ not only speaks of the union of Christ with his people, the whole (catholic) Church, but also implies a conjugal union between Christ and every believer. In the Old Testament prophets, Yahweh courts Israel and betroths her to him. The wilderness journey was seen as the honeymoon period when Israel entered into a covenantal union with Yahweh her husband (Jeremiah 2.2). The sexual imagery is explicit in Ezekiel 16.8 where Yahweh 'spreads his skirt' over the nubile Israel, just as Boaz spread his skirt over Ruth (Ruth 3.9). Hosea came to understand that just as he had married a harlot (or a woman who later became a harlot) so Yahweh had married unfaithful Israel. But he would woo her back and she would resolve, 'I will return to my first husband' (Hosea 2.7; cf. 16, 19). The Isaianic school looked towards the renewal of the covenant when the land would again be married (*beulah*) to the Lord (Isaiah 62.4–5).

Paul picks up this Old Testament theme when he writes to the Corinthians, 'I betrothed you to Christ to present you as a pure bride (AV: chaste virgin) to her one husband' (2 Corinthians 11.2). Ephesians 5.21–33 develops a sustained analogy of Christ as the husband and the Church as his bride. Citing Genesis 2.24: 'For this reason a man shall leave his father and mother and be joined to his wife, and the two shall become one flesh', the writer adds: 'This mystery is a profound one, and I am saying that it refers to Christ and the Church'. Once again, Paul (and the author of Ephesians, if not Paul himself) did not invent this image. In Mark 2.19 Jesus compares himself to the bridegroom, in whose presence fasting would be out of place. Matthew has the parables of the marriage feast (22.1–10) and the ten virgins (25.1–13), while in John 3.29, John the Baptist represents himself as the friend of the bridegroom or 'best man'. It was at the marriage feast at Cana in Galilee that Jesus performed his first 'sign' and 'manifested his glory' (John 2.1–11). Revelation speaks of the marriage supper of the Lamb (19.7–9) and of 'the holy city, new Jerusalem, coming down out of heaven from God, prepared as a bride adorned for her husband' (21.2). All these are corporate images, applied to the whole 'catholic' Church.

But the New Testament also thinks of the relation between the individual Christian and Christ in terms of a conjugal union. First, Paul reminds the Corinthians that just as sexual union with a prostitute makes a man 'one flesh' with her ('flesh' has sexual overtones anyway: the Hebrew *basar* being used of the male member in the Old Testament), so he who is united to the Lord becomes one spirit with him. The Greek *kollao*, unite, join, is used in the Greek translation of the Old Testament (LXX) to render Genesis 2.24: 'a man . . . cleaves to his wife and they become one flesh'. Second, in Romans 7.1–14, Paul develops a subtle rabbinic exegesis to show that Christians have been freed from their obligation to the law through the death of Christ — i.e. they have been widowed — so that they may be married to Christ: 'You have died to the law through the body of Christ, so that you may belong to another, to him who has been raised from the dead, in order that we may bear fruit [children?] for God'. Paul's logic is contorted and, to us, unconvincing, but the image of conjugal union between the believer and Christ shines through clearly enough.

Finally, Ephesians 5 speaks of Christ uniting his bride to himself through baptism: 'Christ loved the church and gave himself up for her, that he might sanctify her, having cleansed her by the washing of water with the word, that he might present the church to himself in splendour, without spot or wrinkle or any such thing, that she might be holy and without blemish' (Ephesians 5.25–27). It appears to follow that it is all the baptized who share in the nuptial union of Christ and his Church.

A *new humanity* has been created by the Incarnation, death, resurrection and ascension of Christ — a new corporate person into which Christians are incorporated by baptism. Following once again the presumed order of writing of the New Testament books, we note first of all Galatians 3.27–28: 'For as many of you as were baptized into Christ have put on Christ' — not as a mere outward vesture but as a new humanity which transcends worldly distinctions and abolishes discrimination based upon them: 'There is neither Jew or Greek, there is neither slave nor free, there is neither male or female; for you are all one [Greek: 'one man', 'one person'] in Christ Jesus'. Paul thinks of a new creation of humanity taking place through our baptismal incorporation into Christ: 'If any one is in Christ he is a new creation' (2 Corinthians 5.17). Christ is a new redeemed corporate and representative humanity, as Adam was the old sinful corporate and representative humanity (Romans 5.6–21), for 'as in Adam all die, so also in Christ shall all be made alive' (1 Corinthians 15.22). Just as in our fallen, mortal humanity 'we have borne the image of the man of dust' (Adam), so in our renewed, incorruptible humanity 'we shall . . . bear the image of the man of heaven' — 'the Adam of the end-time' (vv. 49, 45). Colossians 3.10 reminds believers that they have put off the old humanity (RSV: 'nature'; Greek, *anthropon*, man) and have put on the new humanity 'which is being renewed in knowledge after the image of its creator' (cf. Genesis 1.26), while Ephesians 4.24 urges Christians to become what they are by putting off the old humanity (RSV: 'nature'; Greek: *anthropon*, man) and putting on the new humanity, 'created after the likeness of God'. The Colossian context makes it clear that this putting off and putting on is effected in baptism: 'You were buried with him in baptism, in which you were also raised with him through faith in the working of God, who raised him from the dead' (Colossians 2.12).

Once again we find that Paul (and the writers of Ephesians and Colossians) did not invent this concept of Christ's corporate humanity, but derived it from the tradition that represented Jesus speaking of himself indirectly as 'son of man'. As Richardson comments: 'Paul dispenses with the Semitism "Son of Man" but retains the idea' (p. 138). There is a deliberate ambiguity about 'son of man' on the lips of Jesus. It suggests on the one hand the self-effacingness and anonymity of a man who could be ignored, rejected and eliminated — reminding us of the title of Primo Levi's narrative of the Holocaust *If This Is A Man*, or Lear's 'Is man no more than this?' (III.4.105) when he encounters Tom o'Bedlam (Edgar) on the storm-swept heath. And on the other hand it entails the corporate conception of Daniel 7.14, 27 where 'one like a son of man' stands for 'the people of the saints of the Most High' and its development in the Similitudes of Enoch (that may or may not have influenced New Testament use of 'Son of Man': that remains the subject of intense scholarly discussion). It is significant that this corporate humanity — the eschatological 'perfect man, the measure of the stature of the fullness of Christ' — is identified with 'the whole body' which builds itself up in love, in Ephesians 4.13, 16. In baptism we put on a new human nature by being incorporated into the human nature of Christ which exists on earth as his Church. Hence John Robinson can say, 'The resurrection of the body starts at baptism' (p. 79). It is to baptism — and specifically the baptism of Jesus — that we now turn.

Finally, we come to the key that unlocks the whole mystery of our baptismal incorporation into the body of Christ — the baptism of Jesus himself. It is the deep ontological significance of the baptism of Jesus that makes baptism the sacrament of justification, enabling Paul to say: 'You were washed, you were sanctified, you were justified in the name of the Lord Jesus Christ and in the Spirit of our God' (1 Corinthians 6.11). This alone can explain how the simplest act, employing the element of water, can carry such momentous consequences in Christian theology.

The fact that the tradition that Jesus had been baptized by John presented the early Christian community with a problem (Matthew 3.14f.) gives it the ring of truth. It bears the stamp of authenticity. At his baptism at the hands of John, the preacher of repentance and judgement to come, Jesus decisively entered into solidarity with his people. It is incompatible with New Testament Christology to suppose that Jesus approached his baptism in the same spirit of repentance and conversion (*metanoia*) as the crowds who flocked to Jordan's bank. His action only makes sense if it was an act motivated by a vocation that he already felt, if he took this step as a part of the destiny he had already embraced. In other words, it was as a representative person that Jesus was baptized. His reply to John's challenge: 'thus it is fitting for us to fulfil all righteousness' (Matthew 3.15), seems to be an echo of Isaiah 53.11: 'by his knowledge shall the righteous one, my servant, make many to be accounted righteous' (Flemington, pp. 25ff.; Lampe, *Seal*, p. 37). The suffering Servant of Deutero-Isaiah is a representative, corporate person, just as the Son of Man of Daniel 7.14 is. By this act of solidarity, Jesus is proleptically numbered with the transgressors, bears the sins of many and makes intercession for them (Isaiah 53.12).

Jesus' baptism was then an acceptance of the vocation he had come to know, it was an act of obedience and surrender to the will of God. By it he embraced his destiny. He looked back to what happened then as the source of his authority (Mark 11.30; Jeremias, 1, p. 56). It is implausible to suppose that Jesus saw at this stage all that lay before him — rejection, humiliation, death and resurrection — mapped out in detail, but it is reasonable to assume that his knowledge of scripture gave him the clear sense that humiliation and ultimate vindication was to be his lot. He would have rested trustfully in the will of God to lead him step by step. As Beasley-Murray puts it:

As Messiah, representative of people needing deliverance, Jesus demonstrates and effects his solidarity with them in their need. . . In submitting to the baptism of John, the Lord condemns the self-righteous and the wicked for their lack of repentance and takes his stand with the publicans and sinners, as well as more respectable members of society, who look for the Day of the Lord. It is not for us immediately to turn to the conclusion of the Gospel to see whither this solidarity of the Messiah with sinners would lead him. . . . (p. 60)

As the shape of his destiny became clearer, the significance of his baptism loomed larger and he saw its symbolism of descent and ascent as the prophetic enactment of his humiliation and vindication, suffering and deliverance, death and — perhaps even — resurrection. On the road to Jerusalem, Jesus rejected the *theologia gloriae* proposed by James and John who asked to share his throne in glory, and grimly outlined a *theologia crucis* for himself and them:

> But Jesus said to them, 'You do not know what you are asking. Are you able to drink the cup that I drink, or to be baptized with the baptism with which I am baptized?' And they said to him, 'We are able.' And Jesus said to them, 'The cup that I drink you will drink; and with the baptism with which I am baptized, you will be baptized . . . ' (Mark 10.38f.)

The cup here is not the cup of salvation primarily (Psalms 116.13; 23.5; Matthew 26.29), but the cup of suffering, even of the wrath of God (Psalm 75.8; Isaiah 51.17, 22; Jeremiah 25.28; Ezekiel 23.32ff.; Habakkuk 2.15f.; Revelation 14.10; 16.19), that Jesus in his agony prayed to be spared (Luke 22.42). But is there perhaps a hint of joyful communion in the loving cup when once the cup of suffering has been emptied to the dregs? Similarly the image of baptism implies a rising up out of the waters — the waves and billows of affliction (Psalms 42.7; 69.2, 15; 124.4f.) — to triumph over them and ride upon them as the ark floated above the Flood (1 Peter 3.21f.) Significantly, the passage ends with an exhortation to humble servanthood after the example of the Son of Man 'who came not to be served but to serve and to give his life as a ransom for many' (Mark 10.43f.; cf. Isaiah 53.11f.).

The comparable passage (Luke 12.49f.) sets the reference to Jesus' baptism of suffering in the context of judgement rather than servanthood:

> I came to cast fire upon the earth; and would that it were already kindled! I have a baptism to be baptized with; and how I am constrained until it is accomplished! Do you think that I have come to give peace on earth? No, I tell you, but rather division.

The parallel in Matthew (10.34ff.) omits the reference to baptism, but speaks of taking up one's cross and losing one's life for Christ's sake. Matthew's 'sword' (10.34) in place of Luke's 'division' is probably an indication of authenticity, but Luke's insight into the 'constraint', the pressure, that Jesus experienced as he moved towards the fulfilment of his vocation is also indubitably primitive. The fire stands for judgement and is paralleled with 'baptism'. John the Baptist has prophesied that the coming one would baptize with fire and exercise judgement:

> I baptize you with water; but he who is mightier than I is coming . . . he will

baptize you with the Holy Spirit and with fire. His winnowing fork is in his hand, to clear his threshing floor, and to gather the wheat into his granary, but the chaff he will burn with unquenchable fire. (Luke 3.16f.)

John was the Elijah who would prepare the way before the Lord and warn of fiery judgement to come (Malachi 4.5; 3.1).

But who can endure the day of his coming, and who can stand when he appears? For he is like a refiner's fire . . . he will sit as a refiner and purifier of silver, and he will purify the sons of Levi and refine them like gold and silver . . . . Then I will draw near to you for judgement . . . . For I the Lord do not change; therefore you, O sons of Jacob, are not consumed. (Malachi 3.2–6)

A further connection between the Marcan, Matthean and Lucan references that link baptism, judgement and the death of Christ is found in the fact that in Psalm 11.6 'fire' (cf. Luke 12.49; Matthew 10.34) is paralleled with 'cup' (Mark 10.38):

On the wicked he will rain coals of fire and brimstone;
a scorching wind shall be the portion of their cup.

And the isolated oracle of Isaiah 30.27f. employs the multiple metaphor of fire, wind (breath) and flood for the coming judgement on the nations. D.C. Allison has pointed out that 'in the apocalyptic literature and at Qumran, fire and water are joined to become one symbol' (p. 126).

In the light of the constellation of symbols linking Christ's death with his baptism, Beasley-Murray concludes that the baptism that laid its constraint on Jesus was understood as an enduring of the judgement of God. But Luke implies that Jesus not only suffers judgement, but exercises it: 'casting fire on the earth'. 'The Messiah has come to judge the world and be judged for the world' (p. 75). He pays the price of the judgement he had come to pronounce, and absorbs in his own person the objective alienation of humanity that the Bible calls 'the wrath of God'. The fire was kindled in himself (cf. Dunn, *Baptism*, p. 42) and consumed him (John 2.17).

In his baptism Jesus consecrated himself to his God-given destiny and pioneered the way for his disciples by undergoing baptism as a representative figure. For both Jesus and his people baptism is thus effectively symbolic of suffering and vindication. Just as he humbled himself and became obedient (Philippians 2.8), so too his disciples, then and now, follow their master through the waters of repentance and conversion for the forgiveness of sins (Acts 2.38). Just as the heavens were 'torn apart' (Mark 1.10 – prefiguring perhaps the rending of the temple curtain from top to bottom: Mark 15.38), so Jesus opened up the holy of holies to our corporate humanity in his ascension (Hebrews 9.24). Just as the Holy Spirit was poured upon him, proleptic of his reception of the Spirit when he had been exalted to the right hand of God (Acts 2.33), so too his disciples then and now are anointed as he was, sharing in the messianic office of the representative servant of the Lord (Acts 10.38; cf. 1 Samuel 16.13; Psalm 89.20; Isaiah 11.2; 42.1; 61.1). And just as the heavenly voice declared the Father's good pleasure in the obedience of the Son, confirming and cementing the unique (*agapetos*) and intimate relationship, so too his disciples both then and now receive their adoption as sons (and daughters) and know what it means to have the Spirit of sonship crying out to God with something of the intimacy ('Abba') that Jesus enjoyed (Galatians 4.5ff.).

The true baptism is then the great divine–human drama of redemption, from Incarnation to glorification, in which God incorporated our humanity into his own divine life. The sacramental act of baptism is the vivid and effective symbol of our incorporation into that event, just as it was Jesus' vivid and effective inauguration of his destiny. As T.F. Torrance has written: 'Christ's vicarious baptism was his whole living passion culminating in his death, his baptism in blood, once and for all accomplished on the cross'. Torrance continues:

> At the Jordan, Jesus wearing our humanity was baptized and anointed for us; at the cross, suffering in our humanity, he was baptized for us in judgement and death; and in the resurrection he was clothed with power and raised for our justification. On the ground of his whole atoning act in life and death and resurrection he ascended to pour out his Spirit once and for all upon human flesh, upon the Church, giving it to share in his One Baptism. (*Conflict*, 2, pp. 113f.)

As John Robinson put it in his pioneering study of 1953: 'The baptism of Jesus is his whole existence in the form of a servant' ('The One Baptism', p. 259). Why is it that the New Testament nowhere gives us a description of the rite of baptism? Surely it is because the New Testament is not interested in the rite as such but in the great event that lies behind the rite and gives it its meaning (Torrance, *Conflict*, p. 110). Is this why the fourth gospel stresses that Jesus himself did not baptize (John 4.2), until in his death he baptized all humanity (cf. Lampe, *Seal*, p. 41)?

It was Cullmann who first emphasized the objective, sovereign, prevenient nature of the baptismal event of Christ's saving work:

> According to the New Testament, all men have in principle received baptism long ago, namely on Golgotha, at Good Friday and Easter. There the essential act of baptism was carried out, entirely without our co-operation, and even without our faith. There the whole world was

baptized on the ground of the absolutely sovereign act of God, who in Christ 'first loved us' (1 John 4.19). (*Baptism in the NT*, p. 23)

The beautiful words addressed by the minister to the child at the font in the baptism service of the French Reformed Church (now borrowed by the Church of Scotland) bring out this truth:

> Little child, for you Jesus Christ has come, he has fought, he has suffered. For you he entered into the horror of Gethsemane and the agony of Calvary. For you he uttered the cry, 'It is finished'. For you he rose from the dead and ascended into heaven and there for you he interceded — for you, little child, even though you do not know it. But in this way the word of the Gospel becomes true; we love him because he loved us. (Free translation by G. Yule)

For the New Testament, baptism is not a human action but an objective divine event. The earliest Christians had to coin a new word *baptisma* to indicate this reality and to distinguish it from human acts of ablution (*baptismoi*: Mark 7.4; Hebrews 6.2). Thus baptism was not manifold and repeated but unique and once for all. There is 'one baptism' (*hen baptisma*: Ephesians 4.5) because there is one body and one Spirit, one hope, one Lord, one faith, one God and Father of all. As John Robinson put it: 'The one baptism is that by which the Church is created, before it is that which the Church administers' ('The One Baptism', p. 257).

Christ's redemptive work which brought the Church into being is described baptismally in Titus 3.4–7:

> But when the goodness and loving kindess of God our Saviour appeared, he saved us . . . by the washing of regeneration and renewal in the Holy Spirit, which he poured out upon us richly through Jesus Christ our Saviour.

Hebrews draws a parallel between Christ's baptism of blood which opened the way to the presence of God and our baptism with water that enables us to enter. In 9.14 the blood of Christ purifies the conscience from dead works to serve the living God, but in the parallel 10.19ff. it is baptism with 'pure water' that appropriates the virtue of Christ's sacrifice when he rent the curtain of his flesh. In Ephesians 5.25ff. Christ's giving himself up on the cross for the Church, the bride he loved, is described as cleansing her by the washing of water with the word. Here Christ constitutes the Church by baptism because baptism is the Church's initiation into his redemptive work. In 1 Peter baptismal language of sprinkling, washing and new birth evokes the believer's participation in Christ's cross, resurrection, and ascension (1 Peter 1.2ff.; 3.18–22).

The significance of baptism for ecumenical theology is not far to seek. In the creed we profess our faith in 'one baptism' (*hen baptisma*), not because baptism is unrepeatable in any individual case (though it is); not because the Churches have decided, as a gesture of ecclesiastical diplomacy, to grant recognition to one another's baptisms (though they have); but because baptism is one as Christ is one. 'Baptism is one because it makes one' (Robinson, 'The One Baptism', p. 257). Christians are in communion through baptism into the body of Christ. To deny that fact would be to deny the one baptism, and thus to deny Christ's Incarnation, servant ministry, death, resurrection and ascension — his whole saving work.

However, the question arises whether a denial just as serious is not entailed in our failure to carry through our baptismal fellowship into eucharistic fellowship. For not only is there *one baptism*; there is also *one eucharist* in which Christ is continually offering his people to the Father. Just as the Church's baptisms receive their justification, meaning and integrity from their union with the great Christological baptismal reality, so too the Church's eucharists receive their justification, meaning and integrity from their union with the great Christological eucharistic action taking place in heaven, as the epistle to the Hebrews intimates. Or do we imagine that some Christians and some Churches somehow fail to qualify for inclusion in that ceaseless offering? Reflection on the Christological reality of the Church's life surely compels us to acknowledge that communion through baptism must find its inevitable fulfilment in communion in the eucharist.

3

Communion
in the teaching
of the Churches

The consensus of Anglican theology acknowledges baptism as the basis of our communion

The English Reformers followed the lead of their continental counterparts in teaching that the Church came into being as Christ became present through the word of the gospel and the visible words of the sacraments of baptism and the Lord's Supper. Article 19 of the Thirty-nine Articles of Religion followed the Lutheran Augsburg Confession of 1530 in affirming:

> The visible Church of Christ is a congregation of faithful men, in which the pure word of God is preached and the sacraments be duly ministered according to Christ's ordinance.

The post-communion prayer spoke of the Church as 'the mystical body of thy Son, which is the blessed company of all faithful people' (1662). Here, by the 'faithful' is understood the baptized. The Catechism taught the candidate for confirmation to see his or her baptism as the event 'wherein I was made a member of Christ, the child of God, and an inheritor of the kingdom of heaven' (1549). For the Anglican Reformers, the Church was the body in which Christ dwelt through the dynamic operation of word and sacrament. This dynamic reality was not bound by rubrics, did not need to be licensed by authority and was not the creature of a hierarchy having sacramental grace at its disposal.

The English Reformers rejected the popular medieval notion that confirmation was necessary to salvation. As Tyndale put it, alluding to chrism: 'They think that if the bishop butter the child in the forehead that it is safe' (PS, 1, p. 277). For the English Reformers the fullness of saving grace was given in baptism. Jewell attacks the theory that without confirmation Christian initiation is essentially incomplete:

> They said he was no perfect Christian, that was not anointed by the bishop with this holy oil chrism. This was another abuse. For whosoever is baptized receiveth thereby the full name of a perfect Christian, and hath the full and

perfect covenant and assurance of salvation: he is perfitly buried with Christ, doth perfitly put on Christ, and is perfitly made partaker of his resurrection. Therefore they are deceived, that say no man is a perfit Christian that is not marked with this oil. Else the apostles and holy martyrs were but half Christians because they lacked this oil. (PS, 2, p. 1126; cf. Lampe, *Seal*, p. 311).

For Richard Hooker, the chief architect of Anglican ecclesiology, it was the fundamental baptismal faith that identified Christians as Christians and churches as churches. He invoked the 'one Lord, one faith, one baptism' (I.x.14: 1, p. 252) of Ephesians 4.5 as 'superaturally appertain[ing] to the very essence of Christianity' (III.i.3–4: 1, p. 339). The baptismal faith is 'that vital substance of truth' which distinguishes the Christian religion from others (V. lxviii.6: 2, p. 369). The basic belief in Christ as Saviour is the foundation of the Church and every church which preserves this faith is a part of the visible church of Christ. It is because the Church of Rome 'constantly still persists' in the 'main parts of Christian truth' that 'we gladly acknowledge them to be of the family of Jesus Christ' (Sermon II.24: 3, p. 513; III.i.11: 1, p. 347).

For Hooker, baptism was not a mere badge of Christian identity, but the effectual means of our incorporation — and Hooker's language is as physical as St Paul's — into the body of Christ. Against the Calvinist stress on predestination and election, Hooker pointed out that we are actually 'in God' from the time of our adoption by baptism 'into the body of his true Church, into the fellowship of his children'.

> For in him we actually are by our actual incorporation into that society which hath him for their Head, and doth make together with him one Body, (he and they in that respect having one name [here Hooker, like Calvin, refers to Paul's calling the Church 'Christ' in 1 Corinthians 12.12]) for which cause, by virtue of this mystical conjunction, we are of him and in him even as though our very flesh and bones should be made continuate with his. We are in Christ because he knoweth and loveth us even as parts of himself. (V.lvi, 7: 2, p. 249)

Our union with Christ is then no mere external transaction, as Protestants are sometimes accused (by Bouyer and Mascall, notably) of believing, but a real ontological 'participation of the only-begotten Son of God, whose life is the well-spring and cause of ours': 'No man actually is in him but they in whom he actually is' (ibid., pp. 249f.). Employing an old patristic image, Hooker continues:

> The Church is in Christ as Eve was in Adam. Yea by grace we are every one of us in Christ and in his Church, as by nature we are in those first parents. God made Eve of the rib of Adam. And his Church he frameth out of the very flesh, the very wounded and bleeding side of the Son of man. (ibid., p. 250)

Hooker speaks of the whole Christ for the whole Church and for every part of the Church. But how is this 'mystical conjunction' or 'mystical copulation' (ibid., 9–10: pp. 252f.) effected? It is effected through the sacrament of baptism:

> Baptism is a sacrament which God hath instituted in his Church, to the end that they which receive the same might thereby be incorporated in Christ, and so through his most precious merit obtain as well that saving grace of imputation which taketh away all former guiltiness, as also that infused divine virtue of the Holy Ghost, which giveth to the powers of the soul their first disposition towards future newness of life. (V.lx.2: 2, pp. 265ff.).

But if that new life is begun in baptism, it is continued in holy communion. Hooker believes that he speaks for the consensus of Christendom ('it is on all sides plainly confessed') in affirming that the eucharist is 'a true and real participation of Christ, who thereby imparteth himself even his whole entire Person *as a mystical Head* unto every soul that receiveth him, and that every such receiver doth thereby incorporate or unite himself unto Christ as a *mystical member* of him, yea of them also whom he acknowledgeth to be his own' (V.lxii,7: 2, p. 354).

Finally Hooker summarizes his doctrine of communion — the communion of Christ with God, of Christians with Christ and with one another:

> Thus therefore we see how the Father is in the Son, and the Son is in the Father; how they both are in all things, and all things in them; what communion Christ hath with his Church, how his Church and every member thereof is in him by original derivation, and he personally in them by way of mystical association wrought through the gift of the Holy Ghost, which they that are his receive from him, and together with the same what benefit soever the vital force of his body and blood may yield, yea by steps and degrees they receive the complete measure of all such divine grace, as doth sanctify and save throughout, to the day of their final exaltation to a state of fellowship in glory, with him whose partakers they are now in those things that tend to glory. (V.lvi.13: 2, p. 255)

Four hundred years later, Hooker's remarkable vision of the reality of a *koinonia* that embraces heaven and earth still excels anything that the Church of today, in its quest for communion, can offer.

Hooker's friend and confessor, Richard Field, author of the massive treatise *Of the Church*, teaches that all who profess the saving truth of Christ belong to the visible Church. The divisions of Christendom — between East and West, and between Rome and the churches of the Reformation — are divisions within the one Church. For Field it is the reality of baptism and the accompanying baptismal faith that continues to secure the Church of Rome a place within the visible Church although she has rejected the Reformation (4, p. 527).

Building on the Erasmian distinction between things necessary for salvation and things indifferent (*adiaphora*) — or 'accessory' as Hooker preferred — such classical Anglican divines as John Hales, Henry Hammond, Jeremy Taylor, Edward Stillingfleet, Gilbert Burnet and Daniel Waterland insisted, through the seventeenth and eighteenth centuries, that the fundamentals of the faith, required for salvation and professed at baptism, were the only proper terms of communion within the Church. The union of the Church catholic, perceived Stillingfleet, depended on its making 'the foundation of its being to be the ground of its communion' (p. 53; see further Avis, *Anglicanism*, pt 2).

Frederick Denison Maurice is articulating the same principle in the nineteenth century when he insists in *The Kingdom of Christ*: 'The language that makes Christ known to us is the only language which can fitly make the Church known to us' (2, p. 125). To belong to the Church is to enter by baptism into 'an eternal and indissoluble friendship' with God through Christ. It is our Christian duty to have faith in this baptismal covenantal union and to actualize it in every possible way. Maurice believed that he was bringing out the logic of Luther's theology that had grounded justification by faith on the objective sacrament of baptism: 'You are grafted into Christ; claim your position!' (1, pp. 285, 273).

Successive Lambeth Conferences have insisted, in their messages to their own Communion and to the *ecumene*, on the foundation of the Church in the sacrament of baptism and its accompanying baptismal faith. Lambeth 1920 addressed its historic 'Appeal to all Christian People' to 'all who believe in our Lord Jesus Christ and have been baptized into the name of the Holy Trinity, as sharing with us membership in the universal Church of Christ, which is his Body'. The 1958 Lambeth Conference endorsed this approach: 'All who believe in our Lord Jesus Christ and have been baptized in the name of the Holy Trinity are incorporated into the Body of Christ and are members of the Church'. Coming right up to date, the 1988 Lambeth Conference, in its Pastoral Letter on Discipleship and Ministry, reaffirmed: 'Our fundamental unity with each other and with all our fellow Christians is rooted in our baptism in Christ'. It goes on: 'Baptism is the primary sacrament, it marks us as Christian. It is the common bond for all Christians across the world' (L88, pp. 315f.).

We then see how unequivocally the Anglican tradition has affirmed that our communion as Christians in the Church is founded on our initiation into Christ by baptism on confession of the fundamental baptismal faith. It holds Christ, the Christian and the Church together. It cannot conceive of individuals being in relation to Christ without being accounted part of his body.

The Roman Catholic Church teaches that all the baptized are united to Christ — but it has not yet drawn the conclusions as far as membership of the Christian Church is concerned

In support of the claim that the Roman Catholic Church teaches that all the baptized are Christians, that is to say, are united with Christ and share in his priesthood, I would like to appeal to four principal authoritative witnesses: St Thomas Aquinas, the Second Vatican Council, Cardinal Joseph Ratzinger, Prefect of the Sacred Congregation for the Doctrine of the Faith, and Cardinal Archbishop of Westminster Basil Hume. Apart from quoting the *ex cathedra* pronouncements of Popes, I could hardly do better!

St Thomas Aquinas teaches that all the baptized participate in the priesthood of Christ. This is the meaning of the expression 'sacramental character'. This character is a sort of mark of consecration setting the believer apart in order that he or she may both receive and hand on the means of grace. The unrepeatable sacraments of baptism, confirmation and order each impart a special character. Baptism does not qualify an individual to minister the means of grace to others, but simply to receive them for him- or herself. Nevertheless, because it confers a real participation in the priesthood of Christ it does authorize a lay Christian to administer baptism in an emergency. Thus it is true to say that Aquinas teaches the doctrine of the priesthood of all believers — though he obviously does not draw all the consequences that Luther, for example, would draw.

For Aquinas there would seem to be degrees of participation in Christ's priesthood: the sacrament of order conveys a greater degree of participation than the sacraments of baptism or confirmation. But baptism endows the Christian with all that he or she needs for full participation in the life of the Church. Thus, on Aquinas's premises, one could certainly draw the conclusion that baptism is a sufficient qualification for receiving communion — and this is borne out by the practice of the Roman Catholic Church in communicating children before confirmation. Edward Schillebeeckx cautiously put forward this view in *Christ the Sacrament of Encounter with God*. For Schillebeeckx, by baptism we are incorporated into the Easter mystery of death to sin and life to God. Following Aquinas, for whom confirmation strengthens us for spiritual warfare, Schillebeeckx sees confirmation as our incorporation into the mystery of Pentecost whereby we are 'established in power' for service. 'Baptism invests us with the priesthood of the Church, and confirmation establishes this in power' (pp. 159–66). It is difficult to see how, on this account, confirmation adds anything to the qualification for communion. The significance of this for 'intercommunion' between churches where there is not yet formal mutual recognition of orders, is not difficult to see.

Aquinas was able to assume, to all intents and purposes, an undivided Church. (Rome did not recognize a sister Church, but only scattered Christians in the East after the 'Great Schism' of 1054.) He did not have to ask, are all those baptized into Christ members of the Catholic Church? When, however, the Second Vatican Council drew up its constitutions on the Church and on ecumenism, it had to tackle the question of the status of baptized Christians who were not members of the Catholic Church. The Council unequivocally affirmed that all the baptized are incorporated into Christ, but when it came to ask whether they were also incorporated into the Church, the answer was not so clear.

First then some evidence as to the status of the baptized: The Dogmatic Constitution on the Church (*Lumen Gentium*) states: 'The baptized, by regeneration and the anointing of the Holy Spirit, are consecrated into a spiritual house and a holy priesthood . . . they can offer spiritual sacrifices' (V2, p. 27). Concerning the laity we read:

> These faithful are by baptism made one body with Christ and are established among the people of God. They are in their own way made sharers in the priestly, prophetic and kingly functions of Christ. (ibid., p. 57)

In the decree on ecumenism (*Unitatis Redintegratio*) we find: 'All those justified by faith through baptism are incorporated into Christ' (ibid., p. 345). And again: 'By the sacrament of baptism, whenever it is properly conferred in the way the Lord determined, and received with the appropriate disposition of soul, a man becomes truly incorporated into the crucified and glorified Christ and is reborn to a sharing of the divine life . . . . Baptism, therefore, constitutes a sacramental bond of unity linking all who have been reborn by means of it' (ibid., p. 363).

But when we ask, second, how non-Catholic Christians stand in relation to the Christian Church, we find a disturbing ambivalence. On the one hand, the Council wishes to stretch out the hand of fellowship to non-Catholics; on the other hand, it will not concede that they are full members of the Church. From *Lumen Gentium*:

> The Church recognizes that in many ways she is linked with those who, being baptized, are honoured with the name of Christian, though they do not profess the faith in its entirety or do not preserve unity of communion

with the successor of Peter . . . . They are consecrated by baptism, through which they are united to Christ . . . in some real way they are joined with us in the Holy Spirit. (V2, pp. 33f.)

On the same page we encounter the uncompromising statement:

> They are fully incorporated into the society of the Church who, possessing the Spirit of Christ, accept her entire system and all the means of salvation given to her, and through union with her visible structure are joined to Christ, who rules her through the Supreme Pontiff with the bishops. (ibid., p. 33)

Here we appear to have the novel doctrine that Christians are one with Christ, not through baptism, but through union with the Church's 'visible structure' and 'entire system'!

Unitatis Redintegratio concedes that those 'who believe in Christ and have been properly baptized are brought into a certain, though imperfect, communion with the Catholic Church' (V2, p. 345) and the reality of their sacramental grace is in doubt:

> The ecclesial Communities separated from us lack the fulness of unity with us which should flow from baptism, and we believe that especially because of the lack of the sacrament of orders they have not preserved the genuine and total reality of the eucharistic mystery. (ibid., p. 364)

The very passage of *Lumen Gentium* that refrains from claiming an absolute identity between the Christian Church and the Roman Catholic Church, asserting only that the former 'subsists in' (*subsistit in*) the latter, at the same time makes it clear that the authentic ecclesial components (if I can call them that) found within the separated communities, exist in detachment from the Christian Church:

> This Church, constituted and organized in the world as a society, subsists in the Catholic Church, which is governed by the successor of Peter and by the bishops in union with that successor, although many elements of sanctification and of truth can be found outside her visible structure. These elements, however, as gifts properly belonging to the Church of Christ, possess an inner dynamism toward Christian unity. (V2, p. 23)

I find the same ambivalence present — and accentuated — in Cardinal Joseph Ratzinger's recently published collection of essays on ecclesiology. Tackling the question, 'Who belongs to the Church?', Ratzinger points out that Pope Pius XII's encyclical on the mystical Body of Christ in 1943 prescribed three requirements for Church membership: baptism, orthodoxy and being incorporated into the legal unity of the Church. As Ratzinger comments, this meant that non-Catholics were completely excluded from membership of the Church. However, another strand of tradition, preserved in the corpus of Canon Law, held open the possibility of a more generous view. According to Canon Law, observes Ratzinger, 'baptism provided an unlosable form of constitutive membership of the Church' (p. 15). It was this element in the Catholic tradition, rather than that perpetuated by Pius XII, that the Second Vatican Council chose to develop.

Commenting on the crucial expression of Vatican II, *subsistit in*, the Cardinal will go no further than his text. 'Even outside the Catholic Church there are many true Christians and much is truly Christian.' But this does not affect the unique claims of the Church of Rome: 'The true Church is a reality that exists, even now, without one on that account having to deny that other Christians are Christians or to dispute an ecclesial character on the part of their communities' (p. 120). One of Ratzinger's definitions harks back to that encyclical of Pius XII and the inveterate insistence of the Church of Rome that one must be in communion with the Pope for salvation: 'the Catholic Church, that is the community of the bishops among themselves and with the Pope' (p. 115).

Where Vatican II went so far as to say that the Church of Christ 'is really present in all legitimately organized local groups of the faithful, which so far as they are united to their pastors', are called churches in the New Testament, Ratzinger seizes upon the phrases 'legitimately organized' and 'united to their pastors' to oppose the theology of the Reformers and the Russian Orthodox thinkers in exile that every eucharistic community is the Church because it possesses Christ, and that external unity with other communities is not constitutive of the Church (pp. 8f.).

So while the Cardinal welcomes the degree of unity that already exists through shared belief and through a common baptism, and wants to see this deepened and extended, he deplores protestant pressure to develop this into actual intercommunion. The one sacramental body of Christ is the prerogative of the one ecclesial body of Christ, and 'dissociating the bodiliness of the sacrament from the bodiliness of the Church means crushing both the Church and the sacrament underfoot' (p. 141). It is clear that here the Church has been defined apart from the constitutive efficacy of the sacrament of holy baptism as that whereby we are incorporated into Christ and his priesthood. Ratzinger leaves us with the strange anomaly of Christians sacramentally incorporated into Christ by baptism who nevertheless are debarred from the sacramental expression of this incorporation in another sacrament, the eucharist. But the Prefect of the Sacred Congregation for the Doctrine of the Faith is here representative of a stage of modern Catholic ecclesiology, that of Vatican II, which recognized the reality of the baptismal basis of Christian communion, yet failed to draw the consequences.

In an important essay 'The Church as Communion' Cardinal Basil Hume has highlighted the concept of *koinonia* as pointing to 'the heart of mystery . . . the ultimate reality of the Church' (p. 17). Cardinal Hume is acutely aware of the significance of this concept for the Churches' search for unity. 'There can be little doubt', he remarks, 'that the rediscovery of the richness of koinonia is . . . gradually transforming our understanding of Christian ecumenism. It helps to explain both our fundamental unity which disunity has never succeeded in destroying and to provide us with the dynamic thrust towards full organic unity' (p. 24).

Cardinal Hume underlines the fact that this *koinonia* is based on our common baptism. 'Through baptism we become part of the people of God and members, too, of the body of Christ. . . . We are given new life which we share with all the baptized' (p. 20). He recognizes that this has momentous consequences for ecumenism: 'The mutual recognition of the validity of Christian baptism has profoundly changed the relationships between separated Christians' (p. 24). He contrasts the new spirit of fellowship based on acknowledgement of our common baptism with the ecclesiastical imperialism revealed in Pope Pius XII's assertion in the encyclical *Mystici Corporis* that 'the true Church of Christ' was 'the Holy, Catholic, Apostolic, *Roman* Church' (pp. 24f.; my italics). The cardinal insists that:

> It is now clearly understood — and this is a development not wholly grasped either inside or outside the Catholic community — that Catholics now recognise that when baptism is validly conferred at any time, inside or outside the visible unity of the Catholic Church, the person baptised is incorporated into Christ, is without doubt a member of Christ's body. (p. 26)

However, any euphoria that the reader might be feeling by this stage soon evaporates when it becomes clear that Cardinal Hume is not prepared to give an inch on the traditional claims of Rome. As he puts it:

> I would, however, fail in my duty to unity and to truth if I did not draw attention also to that aspect of Catholic teaching which is uncompromising and uncomfortable. Recognition of God's gifts in other churches in no way diminishes or denies the Catholic Church's claim to uniqueness. (p. 28)

He goes on to cite Vatican II's decree on ecumenism: 'The Catholic Church possesses the wealth of the whole of God's revealed truth and all the means of grace' and is unable to concede the same status to others (p. 28). The Cardinal insists that 'the Catholic Church cannot subscribe to a concept of the Church as a unity shattered into pieces by schism and heresy and now awaiting the coming together of the individual churches to remake the great Church of the future' — though he rightly suspects that this is a notion cherished by many outside the Roman Catholic Church. However, it is not a view that Roman Catholics could adopt without 'fundamental violence to our understanding of Church and our reading of Christian history'. The Cardinal continues: 'We can do no other than affirm again in humility and faithfulness our conviction, stated at the Vatican Council':

> Only through the Catholic Church of Christ, the universal aid to salvation, can the means of salvation be reached in all their fulness. It is our belief that Christ entrusted all the benefits of the New Covenant to the Apostolic College over which Peter presides. (p. 29)

I have to confess that I find the naked juxtaposition of ecclesiological principles in this essay deeply disturbing. Does Cardinal Hume believe that the traditional claims of the Roman Church remain unaffected by our modern rediscovery of the significance of the baptismal incorporation of all Christians into Christ? Does he believe that an ecclesiology that takes its rise from the New Testament conception of *koinonia* can be married to an ecclesiology centred on the concept of the Roman Church as a *societas perfecta*? Does it make sense to affirm that Christians can be 'members of Christ's body' (p. 26) without being members of his Church? Is the Cardinal satisfied with a formula that prevents Roman Catholics entering into communion with those who are themselves, as he seems to recognize, in communion with Christ through baptism? But in all this he is simply being faithful to the teaching of the Second Vatican Council which placed these two principles — the indestructible unity of all the baptized in Christ and the uncompromising claims of the see of Peter — side by side, unreconciled and unintegrated (cf. Tillard, 'The Church of God is a Communion', p. 117). For how much longer, I wonder, can the Roman Catholic Church go on adding two and two and getting the answer three?

The Reformation tradition teaches a real union of Christians with Christ through baptism and the Lord's Supper

A radical recovery of the power of baptism lay at the heart of Luther's Reformation. Baptism is a reality that unites us to Christ and constitutes us his priestly people the Church. Baptism is no mere ecclesiastical rite (as ordination is for Luther — since all Christians are priests by baptism and only need authority to exercise their priesthood) but contains all the fullness of God. As Luther taught in his Large Catechism, by baptizing in God's name, we show that God is the baptizer. Neither the mere water nor the human instrument is important. The water is 'comprehended in God's word and commandment and sanctified by them'. We should therefore focus not on the crude, external mask, like the shell of a nut, but on the reality it encloses — God's word that contains all the fullness of God. Just as at the baptism of Jesus in the Jordan, in baptism the heavens open and reveal the glory of God (*BC*, pp. 436ff.).

> Hence we ought to receive baptism at human hands just as if Christ himself, indeed God himself, were baptizing us with his own hands. . . . The Lord sitting in heaven thrusts you under the water with his own hands, and promises you forgiveness of your sins, speaking to you upon earth with a human voice by the mouth of his minister. (*LW* 36, p. 62)

In baptism, we enter a covenantal union with God through Christ. He comes alongside us and becomes one with us 'in a gracious covenant of comfort'. When continuing sin terrifies us with the wrath of God 'we must boldly and without fear hold fast to our baptism, set it high against all sins and terrors of conscience', claiming, 'I am baptized, and through my baptism God, who cannot lie, has bound himself in a covenant with me'. In the sacrament of penance we re-enter and reappropriate our baptism, appeal again to the covenant, and receive the forgiveness of our sins (*LW* 35, pp. 33–43). The Christian life is therefore 'a daily baptism, once begun and ever continued' and in their baptism Christians have enough to study and to practise all their lives (*BC*, pp. 436ff.).

In *The Babylonian Captivity of the Church*, one of his foundational Reformation writings (1520), Luther deplored the way in which the medieval paraphernalia of vows, good works, penances, indulgences, pilgrimages, etc. had obscured the one way of forgiveness and drawing near to God — the sacrament of baptism. Instead, the comfort of baptism should have been ceaselessly inculcated.

> For just as the truth of this divine promise, once pronounced over us, continues until death, so our faith in it ought never to cease, but to be nourished and strengthened until death by the continual remembrance of this promise made to us in baptism. . . . For the truth of the promise remains steadfast, always ready to receive us back with open arms when we return. (*LW* 36, p. 59)

If we are made one with Christ by baptism, we are made one with all his people in the sacrament of the altar, mass, or Lord's Supper. Luther has an advanced concept of *koinonia*, stressing that the significance or effect of the sacrament is 'fellowship of all the saints' and relating this to the Greek *synaxis* and the Latin *communio*.

> Hence it is that Christ and all the saints are one spiritual body, just as the inhabitants of a city are one community and body, each citizen being a member of the other and of the entire city. All the saints, therefore, are

members of Christ and of the Church, which is a spiritual and eternal city of God. And whoever is taken into this city is said to be received into the community of saints and to be incorporated into Christ's spiritual body and made a member of him. (*LW* 35, pp. 50f.)

This fellowship consists in all the 'spiritual possessions' of Christ and his saints becoming the common property of all who share in the sacrament — not only all spiritual blessings and privileges, but also all the sufferings and sins of the saints which are shared in mutual love (ibid., pp. 51f.). As Luther sums up his conception of communion:

The blessing of this sacrament is fellowship and love, by which we are strengthened against death and all evil. This fellowship is twofold: on the one hand we partake of Christ and all saints; on the other hand we permit all Christians to be partakers of us, in whatever way they and we are able. Thus by means of this sacrament all self-seeking love is rooted out and gives place to that which seeks the common good of all; and through the change wrought by love there is one bread, one drink, one body, one community. (ibid., p. 67)

Calvin and the Reformed tradition share in the consensus of Christian Churches which teaches a real incorporation of the baptized into Christ. Calvin's doctrine of the predestination of the elect to eternal life leads him to discourage the baptism of infants by midwives — there can be little urgency about baptizing the children of believers when we know through God's promises that they are safe in the covenant (*Institutes* IV.xv.29: 2, pp. 524ff.), but it does not lead him to play down the real efficacy of baptism in the case of adults.

The office of the sacraments is the same as that of the word of God — 'to hold forth and offer Christ to us, and, in him, all the treasures of heavenly grace' (*Institutes*, IV.xiv.17: 2, p. 503). Baptism in particular assures us 'not only that we are ingrafted into the death and life of Christ, but so united to Christ himself as to be partakers of all his blessings' (ibid., xv.6: p. 515). Like Luther, Calvin regards baptism as a 'spiritual reality' that remains with us all our lives and to which we may 'flee' for the assurance of pardon when we are oppressed by our sins (*T&T*, 3, p. 182). The popular medieval insistence that confirmation is necessary to complete our baptism and make us fully Christian is a 'sacrilege replete with blasphemy' (ibid., p. 183).

In his understanding of the Lord's Supper, Calvin lacks (at least as far as the *Institutes* are concerned) the 'horizontal', corporate dimension of communion with one another through communion with Christ. His emphasis falls on the real union between Christ and the believer that is set forth and strengthened in the supper. It is 'a testimony that they form one body with Christ, so that everything which is his they may call their own'. This is the 'wondrous exchange made by his boundless goodness' — by becoming Son of Man, he has made us sons of God. The reality of communion with Christ Calvin hesitates to put into words, but he is convinced that what Christ designates externally in the symbols of bread and wine he accomplishes inwardly. Thus 'the flesh of Christ is like a rich and inexhaustible fountain, which transfuses into us the life flowing forth from the Godhead into itself' (*Institutes*, IV.xvii.2–10: 2, pp. 558–64).

John Knox's Scots Confession of 1560 speaks of the role of the sacraments as to seal in our hearts 'that most blessed conjunction, union and societie' which the elect have with their head Christ Jesus. By baptism we are 'ingrafted' in Christ. And in the supper, 'richtlie used, Christ Jesus is so joined with us, that hee becommis very nurishment and fude of our saules' (Schaff, pp. 467ff.).

The Westminster Confession of Faith (1647), following the logic of the divine decrees, speaks of the communion of saints before it goes on to speak of the effectual means whereby that communion is created.

> All saints that are united to Jesus Christ their head, by his Spirit and by faith, have fellowship with him in his graces, sufferings, death, resurrection and glory; and being united to one another in love, they have communion in each other's gifts and graces. (Schaff, p. 659)

Baptism is 'a sign and seal' of the believer's ingrafting into Christ and its efficacy is not tied to the moment of administration but will bear fruit in God's appointed time (ibid., pp. 662–3). It is the office of the Lord's Supper to be a 'bond and pledge' of believers' communion with Christ and with each other, 'as members of his mystical body' (ibid., p. 664). The Westminster Shorter Catechism designates baptism as signifying and sealing 'our ingrafting into Christ and partaking of the benefits of the covenant of grace, and our engagement to be the Lord's' (Schaff, p. 697). The Longer Catechism (Q. 167), in the manner of Luther and Calvin, expands on 'How is our baptism to be improved by us?'

Clearly the Reformed tradition, like the Lutheran, understands the sacrament of baptism as an objective reality that unites us to Christ and to each other, as a fact to be lived in and enjoyed more and more through the Christian life, as the basis of the fellowship of Christians one with another. But what the Reformation Churches believe about their baptisms is inseparable from what they believe about their eucharists. Here too, they insist, they enjoy a real participation (*koinonia*) in the body of Christ. If we accept what they profess about their baptisms by recognizing those baptisms as valid and unrepeatable, can we defend an attitude to their eucharists that seems to call their reality in question by suggesting that they lack the vital ingredient of apostolicity that alone would make intercommunion possible? And does not this make apostolicity itself a candidate for reinterpretation in the light of our deepening understanding of the baptismal basis of *koinonia*?

Orthodoxy has a profound understanding of communion which nevertheless rules out intercommunion

The Orthodox tradition has contributed much to the new theology of communion. The concept of *synaxis* (= Latin *communio*) figures prominently in Orthodox ecclesiology. That ecclesiology is centred on the reality of the eucharistic community, through which we become partakers of the divine nature by 'divinization' (*theosis*). Yet, paradoxically, the Orthodox churches are particularly resistant to the notion of *intercommunion*. Why is this?

Orthodoxy believes itself to be the Christian Church without remainder. Its premise is that there is but one Church. The Church cannot be divided into 'branches' (as Anglicans in the Tractarian tradition, picking up an insight of Richard Hooker, suggested), nor can it be fragmented (Meyendorff, *Orthodoxy and Catholicity*, p. 96). There is no schism within the Church; all schisms are separations from the Church (Ware, *Orthodox Church*, p. 249). In all humility the Orthodox believe themselves to constitute the one, holy, catholic and apostolic Church.

Yet the Orthodox churches have been full participants in the ecumenical movement since the Faith and Order conference at Lausanne in 1927. Some Orthodox churches were founder members of the World Council in 1948 and others joined subsequently. It was the encyclical of the Ecumenical Patriarch 'Unto the Churches of Christ everywhere' in 1920, calling for a rapprochement between the Christian churches leading to a fellowship (*koinonia*) and a world fraternity of churches by analogy with the League of Nations, that gave impetus to the ecumenical movement.

However, the Orthodox lay great stress on the World Council of Churches' own disclaimer (the Toronto Declaration 1950) that membership does not entail mutual recognition of one another as true churches, nor any diminution of a member church's own unique claims. Some Orthodox have always been fretful at the tensions thus created and have insisted that ecumenical statements should refer to the Orthodox *Church* rather than the Orthodox *churches* (Stylianopoulos, p. 223). The Orthodox ecumenical vision is of the eventual reconciliation of the churches on the basis of Orthodoxy — not by submission to a centre of jurisdiction but by adoption of Orthodox teaching and practice. It does not deny the reality of grace outside its borders but insists that 'every partial presence of redemptive grace must find its accomplishment, its fullness in the bosom of the one Church' (Meyendorff, *Orthodoxy and Catholicity*, p. 156, cf. 102). Orthodoxy believes itself to be the sole guardian of apostolic and patristic faith from which all other churches have departed to one degree or another. As Florovsky put it:

> The Orthodox Church claims to be *the Church*. There is no pride or arrogance in the claim. . . . The Orthodox Church is fully aware and conscious of her identity through the ages, in spite of all historical perplexities and tribulations. She has kept intact and immaculate the sacred heritage of the Early Church and of the Fathers. . . . She is aware of the identity of her teaching with the Apostolic message and the tradition of the ancient Church. . . . She is aware of having been ever the same since the beginning. And for that reason she recognises herself, in this distorted Christendom of ours, as being the only guardian of the primitive Faith and Order, in other words, as being *the Church*. (p. 157)

The Orthodox claim for their Church is that it is authentic, unchanging, unanimous, infallible and exclusive.

How then do the Orthodox view other 'churches'? As Stylianopoulos has said, 'That the Orthodox Church is the one, holy, catholic and apostolic Church does not imply that the other Christian churches are nothing' (p. 228). The Orthodox churches recognize the orders and sacraments of the Roman Catholic Church and some of them have extended this recognition to Anglicanism. But as Kallistos Ware has pointed out, this implies, in the Orthodox approach, less a juridical decision — the Orthodox do not see themselves as operating at a juridical level — than a readiness to remove practical barriers to communion once other essential conditions are met (Ware, *Orthodox Church*, pp. 326f.). These other conditions concern *vis-à-vis* Rome, agreement over the Filioque clause of the Western creed and over papal primacy (Orthodox do not accept the Pope's claim to universal jurisdiction and the centralization that goes with it) and over aspects of baptismal teaching and practice. *Vis-à-vis* Anglicanism, the other conditions principally concern the diversity of Anglican belief, and practice — theological comprehensiveness and the ordination of women. The Orthodox do in fact regard the Roman and Anglican communions with considerable suspicion.

The Orthodox Church with its decentralized approach, has never claimed jurisdiction in England and naturally does not condemn the breach with Roman jurisdiction at the Reformation (Fouyas, p. 85). But it does hold the churches of the Reformation to be schismatic in other ways. Protestantism is a particularly aggravated form of the disease of Western Christendom (Khomyakov). The Orthodox do not deny all primacy to the see of Rome, but they reject the notion of a visible head of the Church on earth (Fouyas, p. 127).

They therefore do not accept the authority of those ecumenical councils summoned by the Pope since the Great Schism, including Trent and the First and Second Vatican Councils. On the other hand the Orthodox believe that, as the one true Church, they have the authority to summon an ecumenical Council — though they have never done so since the separation of East and West. The last session of Vatican II lifted the excommunication of 1054 and this was reciprocated by the Patriarch of Constantinople. But, as Meyendorff points out, this gesture of goodwill was specific to the limited excommunications of 1054. As far as Rome is concerned, the Orthodox lie under multiple excommunications on account of the anathemas pronounced by various Western Councils (Lyons 1274, Florence 1440, Trent 1542–63, Vatican I 1870) since 1054. As far as the Orthodox are concerned, Rome has departed further and further from apostolic truth and purity as the papacy has become more absolute and has taken it upon itself to promulgate infallible dogmas (the Orthodox believe that infallibility resides in the whole Church). Thus 'the decision of 1965 does not change anything in the canonical and sacramental relations between Orthodoxy and Rome' (Meyendorff, *Orthodoxy and Catholicity*, p. 168).

Some Orthodox theologians have therefore raised as a matter of urgency, the question of the ecclesial status of separated churches. The Orthodox tradition does not make it easy to reach a conclusion on this question. There are precedents for the Orthodox Church receiving converts simply by Chrismation or the sacrament of penance, thus recognizing their baptisms, and in the case of clergy, their orders. Florovsky has asked what this implies for the status of other churches and for the validity of their sacraments (pp. 158ff.). Stylianopoulos has recently called for 'a courageous exploration' of the location of other member churches of the World Council of Churches within the Orthodox ecclesiological landscape: 'an effort to articulate in what positive sense, wherever possible, a member church possesses ecclesial reality, no matter how provisional or incomplete that reality is' (p. 228).

What then is the Orthodox position on intercommunion? That position is abundantly clear. Eucharistic fellowship (*koinonia*) is the fruit and the expression of a unity that already exists. That unity is twofold: unity in faith and unity in the bishop. As the recent Orthodox–Roman Catholic joint declaration *Foi, Sacrements et Unité de l'Église* underlines, these are assumptions that Rome and the Orthodox hold in common.

First, there must be *unity in faith*, an embracing of holy Tradition.

Since the Orthodox believe that they alone have held the true faith unbroken from the beginning, unity in faith is not a postulated unity in some standard of faith that transcends the diverse traditions of Christendom — it is not merely the trinitarian baptismal faith — but the entire faith in its full integrity. The Orthodox are not interested in a hierarchy of truths (cf. Dublin agreed statement 1984, p. 46), or an essence of Christianity, or the Reformation distinction between things necessary to salvation and things indifferent. For them the faith is the faith that has always been expressed in life and worship (orthopraxy) within the one true community of the Church. Unity of faith means a return to Orthodoxy. The Orthodox have maintained with total consistency, since the inception of ecumenical dialogue in 1920, that full dogmatic agreement is the prerequisite for communion.

Second, intercommunion requires *unity in the bishop*. This rules out any sacramental approach to non-episcopal churches. It means that the Orthodox must be satisfied concerning the 'apostolic succession' of other episcopal churches, the Roman and the Anglican. They have given this recognition conditionally. But recognition of orders in Orthodoxy is not a juridical matter — that recognition of ministries could be withdrawn for *doctrinal* error. The apostolic succession is, above all, a succession of true teaching. It is a further implication of the Orthodox insistence on unity in the bishop in that it excludes the ultimate Roman criterion that Christians and churches are validated by being in communion with the Pope (the doctrine promulgated by Boniface VIII in the Bull *Unam Sanctam* in 1302: 'it is absolutely necessary for the salvation of all men that they submit to the Roman Pontiff': *CF*, 804).

The Orthodox have no room for our modern notion of progressive communion, impaired communion or partial communion. They do not see eucharistic fellowship as a valid means of creating communion. For the Orthodox one is either in communion or out of communion. 'The Bible, the Fathers and the Canons know of only two possibilities: communion and non-communion. It is all or nothing' (Ware, 'Church and Eucharist', p. 556). Meyendorff points out that the Church cannot admit to the sacraments those who reject Christian truth. Like Cardinal Ratzinger he regards intercommunion as a capitulation to relativism and 'a theological disjunction between the sacramental presence of Christ and his revelation as unique truth' (p. 155). As the Dublin agreed statement of the Anglican–Orthodox dialogue put it in 1984: 'The concept of "Intercommunion" has no place in Orthodox ecclesiology' (p. 15).

How can we evaluate this position in the light of the emerging consensus within ecumenical theology that our common baptism unites us in the Body of Christ so creating a fundamental *koinonia* that demands eucharistic expression?

First, it is significant that recent dialogue between the Orthodox and Roman Catholics, at Bari in 1987, reached extensive agreement over baptism, though reservations remain on the Orthodox side. Not all Orthodox participants were able to recognize the validity of Roman Catholic baptism because true baptism can only exist in the Church which alone can transmit the Holy Spirit. Rather than starting with baptism, the Orthodox want to subordinate baptism to ecclesiology and pneumatology. On the other hand, however, the Lima document on Baptism, Eucharist and Ministry has been well received by the Orthodox as a basis for further dialogue. It is a striking fact that the documents of Anglican–Orthodox dialogue hardly mention baptism.

Second, Orthodox have never thought of the Church in juridical terms. The notion of universal jurisdiction and of ecclesial authenticity being validated by a central reference point (being in communion with the Pope) is alien to them. For them the local Church is the catholic Church. The local Church is the Church because the eucharist constitutes the Church (given of course the other criteria of unity of faith and unity in the bishop — the bishop being the guardian of faith and the president at the eucharist). The local eucharistic community is not a fragment of the Church but the whole Body of Christ manifested sacramentally and it embraces the whole communion of saints, living and departed. This local eucharistic community is the *locus* of *koinonia* in Orthodoxy. 'In Byzantine liturgical language, the term *koinonia* ("communion") is the specific expression designating the presence of the Holy Spirit in the Eucharistic community' (Meyendorff, *Byzantine Theol.*, pp. 173f.; cf. Clément, pp. 108ff.).

Third, this local eucharistic community is also the focus of unity. As Ware has insisted in a paper on intercommunion:

> As a eucharistic organism, the Church realizes and maintains its unity through the act of Holy Communion. It is the eucharist that creates the oneness of the Church. Unity is understood not in juridical but in eucharistic terms. Unity is not imposed from above by some hierarchical or administrative centre endowed with supreme power of jurisdiction; but it is *created from within* by the celebration of the liturgy. ('Church and Eucharist', pp. 552f.)

It is with this, its central ecclesiological insight, that Orthodoxy comes closest to the new ecumenical theology of *koinonia* (further evidence of the debt that this broad ecumenical approach owes to Orthodoxy). It is encouraging that Zizioulas has made the reality of *koinonia* in the local eucharistic community the governing concept of his theology of personal relation.

My response is to suggest that the Orthodox are right in what they affirm: the *koinonia* enjoyed by the local church as it celebrates the eucharist is the heart of our ecumenical understanding of the Church and is indeed the foundation on which we can build our hopes for unity. But I also venture to suggest that the Orthodox are wrong in what they deny — in the negative conclusions that they draw from this positive insight — namely that eucharistic communities outside the Orthodox fold do not celebrate true eucharists but schismatic eucharists (Ware, op. cit.) and therefore their eucharists are not celebrated by the Church. I would plead with the Orthodox to open their eyes to the reality of the *koinonia* in other eucharistic communities that know themselves to be the Body of Christ and to find a way of conceptualizing the fact of broken communion *within* the Church. I would respectfully ask the Orthodox to consider the following questions concerning non-Orthodox sacramental communities:

a What is the status of their baptism — is it baptism into the death and resurrection of Christ?

b Have they received the Holy Spirit — have they been baptized by one Spirit into one Body (1 Corinthians 12.13)? If not, how is it that they confess Christ as Lord (1 Corinthians 12.3)?

c Do they form the Body of Christ as believing communities united by baptism?

d What is the quality of their *koinonia* — can it be a true communion with one another without being before everything else a communion with the Father and the Son (1 John 1.3)?

e And when they express and strengthen that *koinonia* in the celebration of the eucharist — can it be separated from, excluded from the one eucharistic action of the risen Christ through his Church?

f And how would the Orthodox evaluate the patently inadequate eucharists of the Corinthian church in the New Testament — that certainly lacked unity of faith (the Corinthians held a number of erroneous beliefs) and unity in the bishop (there were no bishops and discipline and order left much to be desired)? So, even on Orthodox premises, for the sake of argument, do they regard themselves as in communion with the New Testament Church?

This approach suggests that communion is not dependent on full dogmatic agreement or full unity of order, but is grounded, in its essential reality, in our baptismal incorporation into the Body of Christ, and that the eucharistic expression of this solidarity may have many imperfections without being deprived of its validity. In his study of baptism, *Of Water and the Spirit*, Schmemann has deplored the 'absence' of baptism from Orthodox life and called for a recovery and rediscovery of the baptismal reality as 'the source of the whole life of the Church' (pp. 8f., 151f.). The baptismal basis of communion has barely been tried in dialogue with the Orthodox: perhaps it is the way forward there too.

4

The imperative
of communion

Our primary obligation to our fellow Christians is to be in communion with them

With the words, 'Receive one another as God in Christ received you' (Romans 15.7), Paul grounds our mutual acceptance as Christians on our free and unconditional acceptance by the Father through the Son. The *koinonia* of Christians is one of the fruits of justification. We are obligated to extend to one another the identical welcome and acceptance that God has extended to us in Christ. We appropriate that welcome, acceptance and forgiveness through baptism with profession of the baptismal faith. But our baptism brings us into membership of the body of Christ the Church. Baptism is situated, so to speak, at the intersection of vertical and horizontal dimensions of *koinonia*. As Duprey has written:

> *Koinonia* designates the relationship of the believer with the Father through the Son in the Holy Spirit and at the same time the new relation, established as a consequence, between believers. This relation between believers is just as real, mysterious and spiritual as that established with God. . . . When I say spiritual here I use the term in the strong sense: that which belongs to the Spirit, which appertains to a definitive eschatological reality. It is the communion of saints, that is, the communion existing between all those who are made saints by the gift of the Spirit uniting them to Christ. (Evans (ed.), p. 10)

Just as our first Christian duty to God is to 'be what we are' and live in the reality of the baptismal gift, so our primary obligation to our fellow Christians is to actualize this communion in every possible way.

It is this primary obligation that makes it essential to get interconfessional dialogues and any subsequent negotiations into perspective. In a recent booklet, Edward Yarnold has asked, *Can the Roman Catholic and Anglican Churches be Reconciled?* It is precisely the *Churches*, as autonomous bodies with their juridical and administrative structures and dogmatic theological commitments, that are the objects of the process of reconciliation. Individual Christians within the Churches, with certain glaring exceptions, I guess do not need to be reconciled to each other across the confessional boundary.

Between them there is already in very many cases, thank God, that complete mutual acceptance, regard and trust that Yarnold mentions as one of the preconditions of full communion, when the members of uniting churches 'know, respect and love one another as fellow Christians, each side recognizing that the other accepts the values of the Gospel and tries to live by them'. The same indwelling Spirit reaches out to the Father and to our brothers and sisters in Christ. For Karl Rahner it is this 'faith that is lived, that counts before God and brings salvation' — as the same Spirit cries out to the same Father in our hearts — that provides the key to progress in ecumenism and ought to dictate our method (14, pp. 248ff., 266f.; 17, pp. 199f.). As I have argued elsewhere, the logic of the situation that confronts us in ecumenical matters is this: the living Christ through his Spirit in the world has created a fellowship of those who, believing the same gospel and sharing the same baptism, find a grace of unity in their common salvation. Their urgent spiritual instinct is to bring this to full expression in the sacrament of unity, the eucharist (*Ecum. Theol.*, pp. 127ff.). It would be a step in the right direction if ecumenical commissions could make explicit the remaining barriers to inter-communion and subject them to theological critique.

The imperative of communion takes precedence over the imperative of orthodoxy

But should not agreement in the truth come first? Some would maintain that there is a higher imperative than that of communion — the imperative of *orthodoxy*. They would insist that extensive agreement in doctrine is the prerequisite for *communicatio in sacris*. This is the policy of both Rome and the Orthodox in matters of intercommunion. Some of the Protestant Reformers also tended to this view — they were not always consistent with Luther's insistence that 'one thing was needful' and that the essential gospel concerning God's free justification of the sinner was the only article of a standing or falling Church. There are several difficulties with this view.

First, it assumes a uniformitarian understanding of doctrine that goes back to the so-called Vincentian Canon with its touchstone of 'what has been believed always, everywhere, and by all'. Uniformitarianism — the assumption that everything always has been, and always will be the same — lay behind pre-Enlightenment history and pre-Darwinian science. In theology uniformitarianism was tested to destruction by Newman in his essay on the development of doctrine (1845). Burgeoning comparative studies in history and culture have made uniformitarianism totally untenable. As we now realize, there is rich diversity and development within the New Testament itself.

Acceptance of the inevitable pluralism of theology today is not a reluctant accommodation to the perversity of theologians but a recognition of the practical basis of belief that all theology emerges from, and that it is a response to a particular cultural, social and political situation, and is conditioned accordingly.

Second, to maintain that the imperative of orthodoxy takes precedence over the imperative of communion, naïvely assumes that the Church's doctrine is *ideologically innocent*. It closes its ears to the Marxist critique which teaches us that every doctrine is ideological — that it is, to put it at its lowest, influenced by economic forces giving rise to social structures, and therefore serves non-theological as well as theological purposes, legitimating the dominance of some and the oppression of others. Doctrines are human constructs; doctrines are social constructs; and therefore must be subject to continual monitoring and criticism. Orthodoxy is falsely absolutized if it is made an imperative that transcends the imperative of communion and keeps Christians apart.

Third, to insist on the principle of orthodoxy as a definable and enforceable body of doctrine depends on a view of *revelation as essentially verbal and propositional* rather than experiential and personal. To ensure that the divine message is received, this view is compelled to extend divine guarantees not only to the original reception of divine revelation but also to its transmission through history. You have to call in a doctrine of sacred tradition, indefectibility and infallibility. Before you know where you are, your imperative of orthodoxy has become subordinated to a higher imperative, concerned with the nature of the Church and the authority of its teaching office (cf. Avis, *Ecum. Theol.*).

The imperative of communion takes precedence over the imperative of order

Others — this is the official Roman Catholic position — would maintain that the imperative of *order* takes precedence over the imperative of communion. Unification or integration of the Church's structures of ministry and jurisdiction is the prerequisite for *communicatio in sacris*. I find this argument unconvincing.

First, it would be *difficult to justify from the New Testament*. True, 'there is one Lord, one faith, one baptism' (Ephesians 4.5) but as A. T. and R. P. C. Hanson have asked, is it not significant that there is no mention of 'one ministry' or even 'one eucharist'? (p. 11). Does this not suggest that the coming into being of the Church, as individuals were incorporated into the body of Christ by baptism, was not dependent on any officially validated ministry?

Second, the imperative of order invariably implies a particular, *historically-specific concept of order* that is hierarchical, imperial and demands obedience. It implies that the higher a person is in the ecclesiastical hierarchy, the closer he is to God, and that his function is to mediate the grace of God to those lower down the scale (Hill, p. 62). That concept too is an ideological construct that is ripe for psycho-social deconstruction as the insights of critical theory bring their bleak enlightenment, employing the methods of both Freud and Marx, to bear on the psychological and sociological roots of authoritarianism.

As has been pointed out, from a canonical and juridical point of view, you are either in communion or out of communion (Evans (ed.), p. 13, n. 31). It is conceived as a matter of ontological status rather than of praxis with its many modes and degrees of translating theological goals into actuality in the lives of people. The ontological notion of communion is a product of false consciousness. It takes communion to be some sort of metaphysical entity, existing in an ideal, heavenly realm, because God has promised it, regardless of its manifestation in practice. It may also assume that there exists on earth a communion that already enjoys the full panoply of privileges that belong to the bride of Christ — a communion which others can be invited to join, on its terms. If they demur, its fullness of *koinonia* within itself remains undiminished. This notion of the Church as a *societas perfecta* is incompatible with a practical understanding of communion which comes to realization when we affirm, cherish, show solidarity with, and take responsibility for one another. The divine order is not imperial and hierarchical, requiring conformity and obedience, but fraternal, egalitarian and spontaneous, expressed in solidarity and creating genuine community.

Intercommunion should be adopted as the proximate goal of the ecumenical pilgrimage

Jean Tillard seems to imply that orthodoxy and order are prerequisites for eucharistic sharing when he writes:

> Eucharist is not a kind of sentimental happening for two communities which were divided before the synaxis and will continue to be divided after it. When two groups have con-celebrated, sharing the unbroken eucharistic body, they belong to the same unbroken eucharistic community. If afterwards they remain two parallel groups, it means that they gave thanks for something they were not, a *metanoia* they have not yet achieved. . . . Eucharistic 'non-communication' is the logical consequence of remaining schism. (Draper (ed.), p. 29)

But this begs the question by pre-defining communion in terms of orthodoxy and order. It hardly squares with Tillard's own earlier emphasis in the same article on the practical manifestations of communion mentioned in Acts 2.42–46 — learning the faith, table fellowship, prayers and sharing of earthly goods. Eucharistic communion is surely not the crowning glory, the cherry on the cake of fellowship, but the presupposition and ground of these practical outworkings of communion.

The momentum of the ecumenical movement came — and still comes — from the pain and scandal of separation at the holy communion, not from the comparatively trivial discrepancies that some Christians recognize a Pope, or bishops, and others do not, or that the set of official doctrines that some Christians carry with them on their pilgrimage are much bulkier than those that others slip into their knapsacks. A more explicit process of reception and decision than the one we have recently gone through with respect to ARCIC I and its *Final Report* will eventually become necessary. (The ARCIC report on authority was nodded through the Lambeth Conference and reservations were swept aside when a member of ARCIC intervened to assure the Lambeth fathers that Roman Catholic intentions were honourable (no Tridentine inquisitors under the bed) and Anglicans must be trusting. I must confess that I had not realized before that the purpose of ecumenical dialogue was to assess the sincerity of the other side! I hope we can take that for granted. I thought in my innocence that it was a much more hard-headed affair and that the words on the paper actually mattered. I doubt whether the Vatican's eventual response will be without some reservations.) However, when this more explicit scrutiny of the proposals takes place it will become patently obvious that the statement on authority and its structures (I am not speaking of the statements on the eucharist, the ministry, and the first report of ARCIC II on justification, with which I have no fundamental argument) does not actually reflect a genuine, broadly-based convergence on the question of authority and freedom, jurisdiction and devolution, between the two traditions. (Elsewhere I have explained not only why it does not reflect such a convergence, but why it does not at points materially assist it: Avis, *Ecum. Theol.*) That dawning realization will be the moment for a greater realism to enter the discussion and for the question of intercommunion to move to the top of the agenda (with full organic union remaining the ultimate but long-term goal, dependent on the success of certain movements within the Roman Catholic Church, and that success or even survival is by no means assured). If and when intercommunion becomes the proximate goal of the Anglican–Roman Catholic courtship — with no absolute guarantee that the marriage dowry will ultimately be delivered — it will become clearer what the participating Churches want out of the enterprise.

Intercommunion is, needless to say, no substitute for ultimate organic unity. A federation of inter-communicating Churches would not answer to the ecumenical quest for *koinonia*. It would be 'reunion without repentance' (Newbigin, pp. 22f.). As T. F. Torrance has written, the Churches cannot go on proclaiming the gospel of reconciliation 'without acting a lie against it by refusing to be reconciled to one another in the communion of the body and blood of Christ'. But on the other hand it would not do to institute intercommunion if the Churches were to 'refuse to act out the deep implications of intercommunion'. Intercommunion imposes an obligation upon the churches to work out their full reconciliation (*Conflict*, 1, p. 125). Intercommunion should not be regarded as an incentive to going the whole way. It is the way!

Only by being in communion with our fellow Christians can we show that they enjoy our unconditional acceptance in Christ

Ecumenical dialogue — with its creative and critical interaction — can help us to discover our identities as communions of the Christian Church. The dialectic of the process can help us become better partners in the quest for unity. There is surely no harm in the ecumenical tail occasionally wagging the ecclesiological dog — provided the dog knows his name and still recognizes his master's voice! As we take our tentative steps towards unity we can begin to see more clearly what that might mean. The most significant of these steps is what used to be called intercommunion.

As I understand the matter, the biblical imperative that arises from the reality that we are all baptized by one Spirit into one Body, is that we should be in communion with each other. It is in our common participation in the eucharist that we come closest to realizing our Lord's prayer in John 17.2ff. that his disciples might be one as he is one with the Father. It is Paul who makes the connection between the eucharist and unity: 'We who are many are one body for we all partake of the one bread' (1 Corinthians 10.17). It is because we partake of one bread that we are one body, not 'We are one body, therefore we partake of one bread'! The eucharist builds up the body of Christ.

Henri de Lubac has recovered the teaching of the Fathers that *sacramenta faciunt ecclesiam*, the sacraments make the Church. In his *Meditation sur l'Église* he develops a dialectic between two contrasting principles. On the one hand, 'the Church makes the eucharist' (*L'Église fait l'Eucharistie*); on the other, 'the eucharist makes the Church' (*L'Eucharistie fait l'Église*) (pp. 123ff.). In his noted work *Catholicism* he cites the Fathers at length. Augustine exhorts: 'Be then what you see [many grains now united into one loaf] and receive what you are [the body of Christ]'. John of Damascus says: 'If the sacrament is a union with Christ and at the same time a union of all, one with another, it must give us real unity with those who receive it as we do'. According to de Lubac, the Latin tradition is unanimous that 'the result of the sacrament is unity'. He further comments:

> Since the sacraments are the means of salvation, they should be understood as instruments of unity. As they make real, renew or strengthen man's union with Christ, by that very fact they make real, renew or strengthen his union with the Christian community. . . . It is through his union with the community that the Christian is united to Christ. (*Catholicism*, p. 35)

We might recall that Ephesians 4.12 tells us that the means of grace are given 'for building up the Body of Christ'.

These reflections invite the question whether we are going about the search for unity in the right way if we are reserving eucharistic fellowship for the moment when the process is virtually complete. The eucharist is the sacrament of unity. But is it only the sacrament of unity achieved, or also the sacrament of unity in the making? The Anglican–Orthodox Moscow agreed statement (1976) is helpful here. Though the Orthodox would presumably not accept the definition of the Church with which I am operating in this book — as all who profess the faith of Christ in baptism and are thereby incorporated into his body — the joint statement puts forward the principle that 'the eucharist actualizes the Church'. It continues:

> The Church celebrating the eucharist becomes fully itself; that is *koinonia*, fellowship-communion. The Church celebrates the eucharist as the central act of its existence, in which the ecclesial community, as a living reality confessing its faith, receives its realization. (pp. 88f.)

A further question I would like to raise is whether a restricted communion is consistent with the nature of the eucharist, or *whether a closed table is not a contradiction in terms*. In *The Church in the Power of the Spirit* Jürgen Moltmann reminds us that the eucharist is the *Lord's* supper, not something that is the property of any church.

> The Church owes its life to the Lord and its fellowship to his supper. . . . Its invitation goes out to all whom he is sent to invite. If a church were to limit the openness of his invitation of its own accord, it would be turning the Lord's supper into the church's supper and putting its own fellowship at the centre, not fellowship with him. By using the expression 'the Lord's supper' we are therefore stressing the pre-eminence of Christ above his earthly Church and are calling in question every denominationally limited 'church supper'. The theological doctrine of the Lord's supper must consequently not be allowed to exercise any controversial theological function through which Christians are separated from Christians.

Moltmann concludes: 'The Lord's supper takes place on the basis of an invitation which is as open as the outstretched arms of Christ on the cross. . . . It is not the openness of this invitation, it is the restrictive measures of the churches which have to be justified before the face of the crucified Jesus. But which of us can justify them in his sight?' (pp. 244ff.). Again, Moltmann insists: 'The open invitation of the crucified one to his supper is what fundamentally overcomes all tendencies towards alienation, separation and segregation' (p. 258).

Nearly forty years ago in a document prepared for the World Conference on Faith and Order at Lund (1952), the Presbyterian theologian, T. F. Torrance, argued that 'the refusal of intercommunion entails a failure to discern the body of the Lord and an unworthy participation in his body and blood'. St Paul told the Corinthians explicitly that for groups to meet for communion separately is not to hold the *Lord's* supper, but to turn it into a private supper and to create schism in the Church. (cf. 1 Corinthians 11.17–34). Torrance urged that:

> Churches ought to sit down together before the presence of the Son of Man, and together eat and drink the judgement of the death of Christ upon their sinful divisions and compromised histories, in order that together they may be given anew the power of the resurrection to rise above the trammels of the past and to realize the very unity of the one body into which they have been baptized. (*Conflict*, 2, p. 201)

So the question needs to be asked: Is a closed table the Lord's supper? Is a eucharist from which other baptized believers are excluded a genuine eucharist? Is it not rather both theologically indefensible and morally intolerable? If some want to raise questions of 'validity' at this point, could not the validity of a segregated eucharist be equally well called into question? Can we claim to accept Christ as saviour and Lord when we do not give unconditional acceptance to all his people? Is it plausible to protest that we do indeed offer them such acceptance when we do not accept them at the Lord's table, the place of communion *par excellence*?

I have referred to Roman Catholics and Anglicans: what about the Churches of the Reformation, especially the Lutheran and Reformed, and the Free Churches who also stand within the Protestant tradition? The quotations from the Lutheran Moltmann and the Reformed Torrance convey a sense of hurt and dismay. It seems to me that the Protestant Churches have been forced to wait for the rest of us, especially Anglicans and Roman Catholics, to come to our senses, like the prodigal son, and to begin that long, painful and penitent journey back to our Father's house.

If our primary obligation towards our fellow Christians is to be in communion with them, do we not have a special obligation towards those who are willing to enter into communion with us? Not all branches of the Christian Church are willing to enter into communion with us, though we are willing to do so with them. As Rome treats Anglicans, denying their orders and sacraments to be orders and sacraments of the Christian (Catholic) Church, so Anglicans treat the Free Churches. Do we not need to make amends to them for the successive rebuffs they have suffered at our hands (the Anglican–Methodist scheme, the Covenanting for Unity proposals)? It is a tragic mistake to imagine that the Anglican theological tradition will only permit intercommunion with those whose orders and sacraments flow from the historic episcopate. While Anglicanism could not compromise on the historic episcopate as a condition of structural union, because the bishop is the effective symbol of unity, that does not imply any adverse judgement on the ministries and sacraments of other churches. If they are founded on the sacrament of baptism — which enjoys its own integrity independent of episcopal validation — then they are ministries and sacraments of the Christian Church (this argument will be substantiated when we come to the question of communion and ministry).

It is an awesome responsibility to refuse to be in communion with those who seek to be in communion with us and are themselves in communion with our Lord through all the means of grace he has provided.

5

Breaking communion?

Even in this ecumenical age, voluntary severance of communion is not a thing of the past. The scarcely veiled threats of secession from the Church of England over the ordination of women to the priesthood may very soon acquire the momentum of self-fulfilling prophecy — as they have done already in the Episcopal Church of the USA. While the leading figures of the protest movement will be careful not to allow themselves to be manoeuvred into doing anything that they do not want to do, some of their more suggestible supporters may find one day that they have burnt their boats prematurely. To prevent sincere lay people and clergy from being hurt unnecessarily, it is high time someone asked what theological grounds there are, in the Christian doctrine of the Church generally and in the Anglican tradition specifically, for separation on this issue.

Denial of the fundamental baptismal faith is the only New Testament basis for breach of communion

It would be anachronistic to read excommunication as an ecclesiastical sanction back into the New Testament. However, severance of communion is contemplated, and even required, by the New Testament under certain circumstances.

First a temporary suspension of communion may be applied for disciplinary purposes. Paul urges the Thessalonians to 'have nothing to do with' a believer who will not work because he believed that the eschatological crisis rendered all wordly commitments pointless (2 Thessalonians 3.4, 6). This informal sanction is evidently meant to shame him into changing his ways. A similar informal and temporary measure seems to be in view in Matthew 18.15–17 where 'if your brother sins against you' and refuses even the admonition of the church, he is to be treated 'as a Gentile and a tax collector'. In a lost letter to Corinth, Paul had urged the Corinthians to shun the company, 'not even to eat with' a professing Christian who 'is guilty of immorality or greed, or is an idolater, reviler, drunkard or robber' (1 Corinthians 5.9–11). A more severe punishment is envisaged in 1 Corinthians 5.1–5 where a believer who is apparently living incestuously with his stepmother is to be delivered 'to Satan for the destruction of the flesh'. Here we have a kind of excommunication that carries, not legal but physical penalties. Paul clearly expects the man to die (cf. 1 Corinthians 11.29–32). This drastic remedy is for the sake of his ultimate eschatological salvation: 'that his spirit may be saved in the day of the Lord'.

Second, a much more serious and final sanction is called for when the essential Christian faith is being denied. Paul solemnly denounces those who preach 'another gospel' as accursed (*anathema*) — and the curse is meant to be effective (Galatians 1.8). While making some allowance for Paul's proprietorial feelings towards the Galatian church, and even for his characteristic over-sensitivity amounting to mild paranoia, it is clear that what calls forth this judgement — the nearest thing to formal excommunication in the New Testament — is the fundamental denial of Christ's redemptive work by the teaching that salvation comes by fulfilling the works of the law. So, justification is involved here as well as Christology. 'Another gospel' amounts to a denial of the faith that early Christians professed at their baptism. Similarly, the 'antichrist' of the Johannine epistles, who had gone out from among them, was the one who denied 'that Jesus is the Christ' and has come in the flesh, which involves denial of the Father and the Son (1 John 2.18–22; 2 John v. 7; see Barrett, pp. 45ff.). This was evidently a gnostic–docetic denial of the reality of the Incarnation. Once again it is the fundamental baptismal faith that is in question, involving soteriology and Christology.

It seems clear from these passages that — temporary disciplinary measures apart — only what cuts us off from communion with Father, Son and Holy Spirit can be allowed to cut us off from communion with each other in the body of Christ. Duprey writes: 'It is with our brotherhood as with our sonship. Our brotherhood in its profound reality (cf. 1 John 3.1–2) cannot be broken except by such culpable infidelity as will strike at our filial relationship and cut us off from the communion of the Holy Spirit' (Evans (ed.), pp. 7f.).

The consensus of Anglican theology permits separation only when we are compelled to participate in fundamental error against our conscience

The classical Anglican divines — liberals, moderates and High churchmen — are agreed on the heinous nature of schism: separation without just cause. They follow the line worked out by John Hales (1584–1656) in his tract *On Schism* that separation is only justified when we are compelled to participate ourselves in fundamental errors that go against our conscience (pp. 4, 6, 9). For these divines, it is not sufficient that we believe them to be errors: they must be fundamental errors, touching the foundation of faith. Even then it is not enough for them to be fundamental errors: we must be compelled to subscribe to them and to participate in them. In the same liberal protestant tradition as Hales, John Locke (1632–1704) asks in his first letter *On Toleration* 'if it be not more agreeable to the church of Christ to make the conditions of her communion consist in such things only as the Holy Spirit has, in the holy scriptures declared, in express words, to be necessary to salvation?' He challenges those who make conditions of communion things that our Lord does not make conditions of life eternal (pp. 14f.).

The moderate catholic Jeremy Taylor (1613–67) insists in his *Liberty of Prophesying* that 'to deny to communicate with those with whom God will vouchsafe to be united, or to refuse our charity to those who have the same faith, because they have not all our opinions, and believe not everything which we overvalue, is impious and schismatical' (pp. 227ff.). From the same stable of churchmanship, Edward Stillingfleet (1635–99) asks in his *Irenicum*: 'What possible reason can be assigned or given why such things should not be sufficient for communion with a church which are sufficient for eternal salvation?' Christians should remain in their church until it becomes a sin to continue. At what point does it become a sin? When we are compelled, against conscience, to participate in the practice of fundamental errors, or the Church requires us to own them as a necessary condition of communion (pp. 112f.). From the High Church quarter, Daniel Waterland (1683–1740) makes it clear in his charge *Of Fundamentals* that separation is justified only when a non-fundamental point is rigorously insisted upon so that we are compelled to profess error (p. 103).

These mainstream Anglican divines were fighting on several fronts at once. First they had to justify the English Church's separation from Roman jurisdiction at the Reformation. Here they insisted that, under the Roman jurisdiction, English Christians were indeed compelled to be partakers of fundamental error against their conscience. Second, they attempted to show why dissent from a reformed Church of England was uncalled for (though we need to remember that dissent did not usually involve a complete breach of communion since 'occasional conformity' required periodic communicating attendance at the parish church). And third, they had to counter the claim of the Nonjurors that the whole Church of England was in schism because it had accepted William of Orange as its sovereign and supreme governor in 1688 in place of 'the Lord's anointed', James II.

The Nonjuring episode is most instructive. For the Nonjurors the divine right of kings was non-negotiable divine revelation (just as for some Anglicans today an all-male priesthood and episcopate is non-negotiable revelation that the Church — or part of the Church — has no authority to alter). Furthermore, the Nonjurors took the step of separation (they were deprived by statute in 1689) not only on grounds of conscience (as those threatening separation in the Church today over the ordination of women) but to save their souls. Their more extreme representatives condemned the juring Church of England as schismatical and apostate and denied that it enjoyed the means of saving grace. George Hickes (1642–1715) wrote of the conforming clergy:

> They can perform no valid acts of priesthood: their very prayers are sin: their sacraments are no sacraments: their absolutions are null and void: God ratifies nothing in heaven which they do in his name upon earth: they and all that adhere to them are out of the Church. (Rupp, *Religion in England*, p. 14)

Similarly, when Newman, Manning and others left the Church of England for Rome in the 1840s and 1850s they did it not as a mere matter of preference, nor even because they were conscientiously opposed to certain aspects of Anglicanism, but because they had come to doubt whether salvation was assured in the Church of England. They were operating on two ecclesiological premises that they had inherited from patristic and Reformation ecclesiology. First, that there was no salvation outside the (visible) Church (*extra ecclesiam nulla salus est*). And second, that there was but one (true) Church. As far as they were concerned, they were not breaking communion with the Church of England, for they had come to believe that it was no true communion. On the other hand, the most distressing aspect of *current* secessions from Canterbury to Rome is that they involve going out of communion with one's Anglican brothers and sisters.

The position of the extreme Nonjurors and the extreme Tractarians does indeed seem to be the only unassailable basis for separation. If you believe that your soul will be imperilled unless you separate, your duty is clear. But these voices were in the minority. The moderate Nonjurors, represented by Henry Dodwell (1641–1711), accepted that the juring bishops of the continuing Church of England, because they stood in the apostolic succession, had a genuine sacramental ministration, even if an irregular one. Their schism, though heinous, had not put at risk the salvation of their flocks. It was not tantamount to total apostasy. These more charitable assumptions enabled Dodwell to lead the return of the first group of Nonjurors to be reconciled in 1710.

Similarly, the moderate Tractarians, Keble, Pusey, Palmer, and others, did not accept Newman's conclusion that salvation was only assured in the Church of Rome. They believed that they could save their souls perfectly adequately in the Church of their baptism. While maintaining with all catholic Christendom that salvation was only to be found within the visible Church, they did not accept the concept of the 'one true Church'. Their branch theory of the Church enabled them to recognize the Anglican, the Roman and the Eastern Churches as catholic Churches. Schism, therefore, could never be justified except when a Church ceased to be a Christian Church and became totally apostate, a synagogue of Satan, as Palmer wrote. On any lesser grounds separation was 'a sin against our brethren, against ourselves, against God; a sin which, unless repented of, is eternally destructive of the soul' (1, pp. 64, 54). Newman and Keble drew opposite lessons from the Donatist schism against which Augustine had contended. While the Anglican Newman came to see himself as a latter-day Donatist who needed to be reconciled to the whole Church, and had given up the branch theory of the Church, Keble concluded that to take such a step would be to repeat the Donatist schism on purist grounds. For Keble 'no amount of faultiness of church governors can make separation cease to be schism'. If the Church of England were to enact 'unlawful' terms of communion, he would contemplate relapsing into 'lay communion' (pp. 393f.).

It is because current threats of separation are not, and cannot plausibly be grounded on the need to save one's soul and do not involve the complete unchurching of the communion of one's baptism that they must be designated schismatic. They cannot even claim the posthumous approval of the fathers of the catholic revival in Anglicanism, the Oxford Movement.

The ordination of women to the priesthood or their consecration to the episcopate is not a valid reason for breaking communion

As we have seen, the grounds on which separation was held to be justified have been well rehearsed in Anglican theology since the Reformation. A breach of communion was only justified where erroneous doctrines and practices were imposed on the conscience as necessary to salvation and/or as conditions of church communion. Now Anglicanism is understandably reticent about laying down the minimum conditions of salvation, believing that only the Lord knows those who are his and that it is incumbent upon us, not to speculate about divine mysteries, but to follow the light we have and to walk in the path of obedience. That is to say, Anglicanism holds out the invitation of the gospel and insists that nothing not clearly taught in scripture may be added as a condition of salvation (Thirty-nine Articles: 6, 20, 21). Correspondingly, its terms of church communion are simply the trinitarian baptismal faith of Christianity — the 'one Lord, one faith, one baptism' of Richard Hooker.

A further form of subscription is indeed required of bishops, priests and deacons. In the Church of England bishops affirm and declare their 'belief in the faith which is revealed in the holy scriptures and set forth in the catholic creeds and to which the historic formularies of the Church of England bear witness', while priests and deacons merely profess to 'accept the holy scriptures as revealing all things necessary for eternal salvation through faith in Jesus Christ' and to 'believe the doctrine of the Christian faith as the Church of England has received it' (ASB Ordinal). But no one in a Church of England or any other church of the Anglican Communion ordaining women to the priesthood or the episcopate is, or will be, required to renounce their conviction that holy orders are reserved, by divine appointment, to the male sex, or to subscribe to the theological principles that lead some to argue for women's ordination. No one will be compelled to receive the ministrations of women priests or bishops. No bishop will be obliged to ordain them. The consciences of those compelled to register their dissent against these developments will be fully respected.

It is therefore apparent that the grounds on which the classical Anglican divines were prepared to justify or tolerate schism are not being met in the present case. There is no principle in the Anglican understanding of the Church that could be appealed to, to justify secession on this issue. It is not merely a question of lack of precedent: there is an ecclesiological principle at stake — the principle that no one should break communion over an issue that is not a condition of that communion. Our communion is based on our common baptism and no developments in the doctrine or practice of the ministry can plausibly be claimed as threatening that.

The Church of England's bishops do not, as a body, appear to appreciate this principle. In their report *The Ordination of Women to the Priesthood* (1987: pp. 20, 26f.), they were too indulgent in suggesting that conscientious objectors to the ordination of women 'would be entitled to explore . . . other ways of continuing their existence within the universal Church'. Better piecemeal arrangements for individuals, they judged, than organized schism! I am aware that this concession may have been necessary to obtain unanimity on the bench, but it gives succour to an ecclesiology that is neither Anglican nor ecumenical. Have the bishops asked themselves what grounds there are, in the Anglican understanding of the Church, for separation on this issue? Unjustified separation — i.e. schism — has been the bane of Church history. The ecumenical movement is attempting to repair the damage, heal the wounds, and create the climate of Christian thinking where schism becomes obsolete as a weapon of ecclesiastical diplomacy. As the Eames Commission (p. 12) put it:

> The same principles which we have painfully learned in the modern ecumenical movement must now be applied to internal Anglican division. The first prerequisite for ecumenical dialogue is the mutual recognition of the partners as belonging together in the one Body of Christ through faith and baptism. From this it follows that what the partners have in common is more important than what divides.

Current threats of secession undermine all that we have gained in recent years in our understanding of the true basis of Christian unity. The bishops do not ask, in their report, what ecclesiological principles are at stake here.

The bishops' suggestion that separation is a legitimate option for dissenters would be underwritten and given symbolic expression, so to speak, by any proposal to make financial provision for those who resign their Anglican orders. But if there are no theological grounds for breaking communion on this issue, any proposal to give what amounts to compensation would itself contravene theological principle. Moreover, it would set a precedent that could be appealed to at every subsequent crisis. For example, what would happen if the Church of England achieved intercommunion with the Roman Catholic or the protestant Churches? Would dissenting Anglican protestants and Anglo-Catholics, respectively, be offered damages?

What concessions then would a theology of communion permit? In my view, these concessions would have to be limited to protecting congregations and individuals from having the ministrations of *a person they could not recognize as a bishop or priest* thrust upon them. If they genuinely believed that in the created order of things a woman was inherently incapable of receiving priestly orders, or that a branch of the Christian Church lacked the authority to extend the ministry to women, so that its orders, when conferred on women, were simply ineffective or invalid, and yet at the same time, on the principles already rehearsed, they were not entitled to go out of communion with others on this score, some provision would have to be made for their pastoral and sacramental care. Two proposals are in the air and have been discussed in the Eames report and by the Anglican primates' conference: they are a structure of 'parallel jurisdictions' and a system of 'episcopal visitors'.

Parallel jurisdiction would involve dual episcopal oversight within a diocese. It would permit parishes to go out of communion with their bishop and transfer themselves to the jurisdiction of a bishop of another diocese. The early Fathers would undoubtedly turn in their graves at the suggestion that clergy and laity could be out of communion with their bishop and refuse to acknowledge the bishop's oversight. They are not required to believe all that their bishop believes, or to approve all that their bishop does, but they are required to be in communion with him (or her) and to render canonical obedience. The Eames Commission was, therefore, right to dub this proposal 'institutional schism'. I suspect that its advocates are tacitly operating with an eclectic, gathered concept of the Church, where individuals opt into the fellowship that seems most congenial on grounds of churchmanship, regardless of historic parish boundaries co-extensive with the parameters of community identity, and that they are then extrapolating this to episcopal oversight. But when it is applied to the territorial concept of the Church it is much less sustainable. It would mean that a bishop could not administer his or her diocese according to a coherent plan and strategy. The authority of the bishop and the integrity of the diocese would be undermined.

Episcopal visitation, on the other hand, would be designed simply to provide episcopal sacramental acts, such as confirmation, by an acceptable bishop (i.e. a bishop recognized to be a bishop) but with the approval of the ordinary, the diocesan. As the Eames Commission acknowledges, this itself would be an anomaly — but one preferable to schism. For it is at least an anomaly that can appeal to the traditional distinction between power of order (*potestas ordinis*) — that is, sacramental power of consecration, etc. — and power of jurisdiction (*potestas jurisdictionis*) — that is, the power to make and enforce measures for the government, oversight and pastoral care of the Church. The Anglican Reformers used this distinction in defending their doctrine of the godly prince as supreme governor of the Church. While emphatically denying to Henry VIII or Elizabeth I the sacramental power of order, they were bound to acknowledge that the sovereign exercised power of jurisdiction in his or her own domains and was the source of magisterial authority in bishops. If the Reformers could accede this purely administrative authority to a lay person, could objectors to women bishops accede it to a woman bishop to save the Church from schism?

One point needs to be made abundantly clear: these 'protective measures' would only apply *where the bishop was a woman* and therefore not recognized by some *as a bishop*. They would not apply in a situation where a male bishop had taken part in the consecration of a woman to the episcopate or the ordination of women to the priesthood. To claim this sort of participation as grounds for breaking communion is to invoke a primitive notion of guilt by association — almost of taboo. If a bishop has taken part in these services, that does not make him any less a properly authorized bishop who is entitled to canonical obedience. As for the scenario sometimes envisaged of individuals excommunicating not only a woman bishop but also all those clergy she will ordain, all those she and they will confirm, and all in the *ecumene*, the whole Christian world, who remain in communion with any of them—that is blatant and aggravated schism and should be condemned in every way.

It is salutary to remember that it is baptism that first brings us into communion with the body of Christ. But baptism can be administered, according to catholic tradition, by lay persons. (The Council of Florence ruled in 1439 that 'in case of necessity, not only a priest or a deacon, but also a layman, or a woman, or even a pagan or a heretic may baptize, provided he observes the Church's form and intends to do what the Church does': *CF* 1414.) Furthermore, as we shall see in the next chapter, baptism is itself a sufficient qualification for receiving holy communion and is our ultimate mandate for all forms of ministry in the Church. So where the foundational sacrament of baptism continues, the Church continues. And if the Church continues, acts of excommunication, other than temporary pastoral sanctions, are self-condemned as schismatical.

In conclusion: there may well be laity and clergy in genuine perplexity, who would be grateful for guidance as to the circumstances in which conscientious separation is permissible. I would submit that the extension of holy orders to women, with safeguards for conscientious objectors, is not one of them.

A branch of the Christian Church has authority to reform its ministry by admitting women to holy orders

This is not the place to embark on a discussion of the merits of the case for opening holy orders to women (on this see Avis, *Eros and the Sacred*), but it is relevant to our study of communion to ask whether a branch of the Christian Church has the authority to break with tradition in this matter. There are some who believe that such a departure from universal tradition would be a schismatic act and would justify separation from the offending body in order to reunite oneself with the catholic Church. Within this broad position, various nuances can be discerned.

First, it may be held that neither the whole Church nor any part of it can *ever*, in the nature of the case, acquire the authority to ordain women. This is the official position of the Roman Catholic Church as expressed in the 'Declaration on the Admission of Women to the Ministerial Priesthood' (*Inter insigniores*), promulgated by the Sacred Congregation for the Doctrine of the Faith in 1976. This statement makes it perfectly clear that the Church (here of course the whole Church and the Roman communion within it are synonymous) 'does not consider herself authorized to admit women to priestly ordination'. The Church simply has no discretion in the matter. Women are excluded from the priesthood, first on grounds of their created nature, since there must be a 'natural resemblance' between the priest and Christ, a man; second, on grounds of our Lord's example in deliberately choosing only men as his apostles, although he broke with convention in other ways in his dealings with women; and third, because the tradition of the Church is universal, unanimous, and unbroken and has therefore a 'normative character'. It is significant that the declaration admitted that this was an issue that 'classical theology scarcely touched upon' and that the magisterium had not pronounced on it before since it felt no need 'to intervene in order to formulate a principle which was not attacked, or to defend a law which was not challenged' (Flannery, pp. 331–45).

This argument from silence provokes the rejoinder that tradition is not a blank cheque on which one can write an imprimatur for anything that has merely been taken for granted and remained unquestioned in dogmatic slumber for centuries. As Rahner points out in his critical response to the declaration, not all tradition is necessarily a vehicle of divine revelation and therefore definitive and binding on the Church. There is also, he argues, a 'purely human' tradition which offers no guarantee of truth, even if it has long gone unquestioned (20, pp. 35ff.).

In his response to the Archbishop of Canterbury, following the Lambeth Conference 1988, Pope John Paul II effectively reiterated the position expressed in *Inter insigniores*. The ordination of women to the priesthood and the episcopate in some Anglican provinces would 'effectively block the path to the mutual recognition of ministries'. The Pope went on: 'The Catholic Church, like the Orthodox Church and the Ancient Oriental Churches, is firmly opposed to this development, viewing it as a break with tradition of a kind we have no competence to authorize' (Eames, pp. 37f.).

As long as the Roman Catholic Church holds that the Church can never, in principle, reverse this universal binding tradition that excludes women from the sanctuary, it is either naïve or disingenuous for others to protest that the Church, or a part of it, cannot break with tradition *until* an ecumenical consensus exists. While the position stated in *Inter insigniores* stands, there can never be such a consensus.

However, there are those who hold, however illogically, that the ordination of women is not excluded in principle and that the whole Church, perhaps convened in a general, ecumenical council, has the authority to break with universal tradition. This seems to be the position adopted by Cardinal Hume in a recent book. It is encouraging that he insists that the Church should be in the vanguard of those who are working for the dignity and equality of women. It is salutary that he notes that significant members of women are leaving the Church and admits that unless the Church does take steps to implement the dignity and equality of its women, it may find that it is too late. However Cardinal Hume also observes that recent Popes have insisted that this is not an open question and that there are no grounds in scripture, theology or tradition for admitting women to holy orders. What then are we to make of this remark?:

> Throughout the present controversy within the Church of England I have consistently argued that this is a step of such gravity and one which is at such variance with the constant practice of the Catholic and Orthodox churches throughout the whole of Christian history, that it should not be taken without the prior agreement of the whole Church. (Hume, pp. 59f.)

Let us be clear: if Popes have insisted that the ordination of women can never be sanctioned by the Church (the Orthodox Churches, though lacking a central magisterium to articulate their position, are in agreement with Rome on this point), then it is highly misleading to talk as though there existed any possibility of an ecumenical consensus one day giving authority for this step. Anglicanism is compelled to draw the conclusion that gestures of ecumenical goodwill are futile and that waiting will solve nothing. The Anglican Communion must either ordain women without Rome and the Orthodox, or not at all. This brings us to the crucial question for Anglicans: Does a part of the Christian Church possess the authority to depart from universal tradition on this point?

The late Gareth Bennett, who I am convinced appreciated the truth of the ecumenical situation as I have outlined it, offered three criteria by which the Church might judge whether a major departure from tradition was justified. His first criterion is:

> Change must emerge out of a genuine crisis in which Gospel and Church are seen to be at stake. The challenge must be a radical one which calls in question the validity of an existing expression of the message or the community and demands a response. It must stem from a wide concern within the Christian community and not from some sectional or particular interest. (p. 133)

In the present case, as I have argued elsewhere (*Eros and the Sacred*), the critique of the patriarchal structure of the Christian tradition, that the insights of the social sciences have now made possible, by exposing the way in which male dominance has allowed male values to be projected on to the transcendent, thus legitimating the inferiority and oppression of women, has precisely provoked such a crisis of the integrity of the Gospel and the Church. It is inescapably clear to many of us that the crisis cannot be overcome until the Church takes decisive symbolic action to demonstrate the dignity and equality of women (to use Basil Hume's words), by inviting them to take their rightful place in the Church's ministry.

Bennett's second criterion is that this challenge 'must lead on to a process of reflection on the nature of Gospel and Church in order to renew their expression and must not have the character of a struggle for power among groups of sects' (p. 133).

In the present case, a profound process of reflection is indeed being generated by theology that has taken to heart the 'feminist' critique of patriarchal religion. For example, there has been a recovery of the true humanity of Christ as we have been reminded that the Word became *homo* not *vir*, human not male. Fresh insight into the gospel has been generated as we have been compelled to face up to the feminist challenge to the catholicity of the gospel and the Church: can they accommodate the aspirations of women who are coming to a new consciousness of their identity, dignity and value? In response, new forms of expression, centring on an androgynous Christology and a concept of God that transcends masculine and feminine stereotypes, are coming to birth. Of course there is a power struggle: as an historian, a synodsman and a don, Bennett knew all too well that major changes could never come about in the Church or any other body without some seeking power that had been denied them and others attempting to hold on to the power of which they had enjoyed a near monopoly. As Stephen Sykes has consistently reminded us in his writings on authority, power struggles go back to the New Testament itself: the Church has to learn to discern and apply the gospel in the midst of conflict, argument and competition. There will never be a power-free vacuum in which saintly scholars can reflect contemplatively on the nature of the gospel and the Church. Bennett seems to acknowledge this in his third point.

Third, then, Bennett suggests that though this challenge may initially involve controversy and division between Christians, 'there must emerge a process of convergence and reception', leading to an expression of 'the mind of the Church'.

This is not really a criterion for deciding whether a change ought to be made, but a pointer to whether, in retrospect, the change was desirable. You obviously cannot have convergence and consensus until someone has taken the initial step. You cannot have reception until there is something to receive. As I have argued elsewhere (Avis, *Ecum. Theol.*), the notion of reception, a post-Vatican II concept that is deployed extensively in the work of ARCIC I and seems to have been eagerly grasped by the Lambeth Conference 1988 as a mechanism for coping with irreconcilable differences over the ordination of women, is the Achilles heel of contemporary ecumenical theology. It is a relic of the uniformitarian outlook of pre-Enlightenment monolithic Christendom. Galloping pluralism in the Church today undermines all realistic hope of an explicit consensus.

Even while the Churches are discovering more and more common ground in their fundamental grasp of the Christian faith, through ecumenical interaction and dialogue, their divergences of practice in response to vastly different situations and challenges are continually widening. If there is a 'mind of the Church', it exists, as Polanyi would say, in the tacit dimension: it is intuitively known and implicitly expressed. Thus all Churches may agree about the need to affirm the dignity and value of women in the sight of God, but this will lead some — those in the developed world — to ordain women to the priesthood and the episcopate, while it leads others — in the Third World — to judge, as St Paul did, that contemporary mores will not permit women to hold positions of leadership and authority. They will attempt to implement their convictions by combating such oppressive practices as female circumcision, bonded labour and child brides. Here the Anglican Communion, which devolves authority to its provinces, has the advantage over the centralized Roman Communion, which still tends to operate on the uniformitarian assumption that there must be one rule for all contexts. As far as the West is concerned, however, there is undoubtedly a convergence and consensus emerging as to the rightness of admitting women to holy orders — though it is largely a *lay* consensus (including theologians and religious). In the Anglican Communion the voice of the laity is heard through the synodical apparatus, but in the Roman Communion the laity have no acknowledged voice. Is a consensus only a consensus when the magisterium agrees with it?

Fourth, Bennett suggests that when a development has been 'received' there needs to be 'some formulation of it by appropriate public authority so that it may be accepted as a norm to be acted upon' (p. 134).

This seems to betray a lapse into the intellectualist fallacy that a 'development' can exist merely at the level of ideas — in articles, books, reports and synodical resolutions — and come in that disembodied state before 'appropriate public authority' for decision, after which it may be implemented with a clear conscience. If Bennett means, as I suspect he does, that a major development, such as the admission of women to holy orders, needs the approval of the *universal* Church, through some organ constituted for the purpose, such as an ecumenical council, then I believe that to be a recipe (and probably an intentional one) for the indefinite maintenance of the *status quo*. There is not the faintest chance of an ecumenical council between Churches who do not even recognize each other's orders or claims to jurisdiction. Those who propose to defer the ordination of women for decision of an ecumenical council are being hopelessly unrealistic and wilfully romantic about the catholicity of the Church. No, this is a decision that every branch of the Christian Church has the authority to take for itself, for the following reasons:

1 *The Church of Christ empirically exists in plurality,* or as Hooker put it, in 'a number of distinct societies, every one of which is termed a church within itself' (III.i.14: 1, p. 351). Later Anglican ecclesiology developed this into the 'branch theory' of the Church. Any decisions that need to be taken, can only be taken by individual churches and can only bind those churches. If the issues are not tackled by those churches, they will not be tackled at all. As Newman first taught us, to live is to change; to fail to change is to stagnate and die.

2 *Ecclesial identity conforms to the contours of human identity.* It is shaped by social, political and geographical realities (see further, Avis, *Anglicanism*, chs 1 and 18). It is sometimes suggested that the New Testament recognizes only two parameters for ecclesial identity: universal and diocesan — and that these should constitute the levels at which responsibility is assumed and decisions are taken. However, it would be difficult to support this from the New Testament. Obviously there were no dioceses in apostolic times, for there were no bishops as we know them. It would also be difficult to show that there was any sense of global identity, of universality. Where the concept of the catholicity of the whole Church does emerge in Ephesians and Colossians it refers to the mystical bride or body of Christ, not to a hierarchical and juridical entity. But neither can the binary scheme of episcopal see and ecumenical councils be read back neatly into the patristic period. For between these two levels, as it were, there stood, by the sixth century, the various patriarchates (Rome, Alexandria, Antioch, Constantinople and Jerusalem) with their metropolitans under them. But this now represents only a tiny enclave of the whole world, the *ecumene*. It is difficult to see how it could be extrapolated to cover the New World and the Third World. The global concept of the Church is a modern one and it is anachronistic to read it back into the New Testament or the patristic period. The concept with which we work today in ecumenical theology is again a twofold one: *provinces within communions*. This concept can claim as much, or as little, biblical and patristic support as the other.

3 *Provinces within communions have the right, and the duty, to reform themselves.* In the sixteenth century local Churches — and in some cases, as in England, national Churches — took in hand the reform of abuses that the papacy showed no inclination to tackle and that the conciliar movement had failed to achieve. When it is argued,

as for example by Pope John Paul II in his post-Lambeth 1988 response to the Archbishop of Canterbury and by Cardinal Hume in a recent book, that only the whole Church has the authority to undertake a change as important as the ordination of women, and that parts of the Church (particular Churches) lack such authority, this is nothing new. In the sixteenth century Rome argued that particular (local, national) Churches lacked the authority to reform themselves without papal approval. This meant that the English Church, for example, had no power to restore communion in both kinds to the people, institute the liturgy in the vernacular, make the scriptures available to the people, also in the vernacular, and abolish compulsory celibacy for the clergy — to mention only those reforms that would find wide support among those 'catholic' Anglicans who insist that the Church of England has no power to ordain women without the approval of Rome and the Orthodox. It is of course still the Roman position that the Church of England had no right to undertake these reforms, which we have taken for granted for 450 years, unilaterally — even though most of them have now been adopted by Rome itself. Would those who doubt the Church of England's authority to ordain women also doubt its right to reform itself in the sixteenth century? It is extremely difficult to see how one could deny the rightness of the Reformation in principle (which is not the same as condoning all that was done in the name of reform) while remaining an Anglican. But then some may wish to object that the ordination of women is not a reform of the ministry but strikes at the heart of the Church's integrity. This deserves our separate attention.

4   *Admitting women to the historic threefold order of the Church's* ministry is a reform of the ministry — of the human, worldly, social and political aspects of the Church's life — not a betrayal of the *esse* of the Church. The early Anglican Reformers operated with the Erasmian and Melanchthonian distinction between things necessary to salvation and things indifferent (*adiaphora*). For them the whole area of the external government of the Church was an *adiaphoron*. Here the Church might properly be guided by what was convenient and edifying or had been ordained by the magistrate, provided it was not contrary to scripture or imposed on the conscience as affecting one's standing *coram Deo*. Even Hooker, though he preferred to speak of 'things accessory', rather than 'things indifferent', distinguished between 'things of external regiment in the Church and things necessary unto salvation' (III.iii.4: 1, p. 357). Things indifferent or accessory should be complied with for the sake of the peace of the Church. It is one these presuppositions that the Thirty-nine Articles insist that 'every particular or national church hath authority to ordain, change, and

abolish ceremonies or rites of the Church ordained only by man's authority, so that all things be done to edifying' and that the Church 'hath power to decree rites or ceremonies, and authority in controversies of faith' (Articles 34, 20).

A challenge to the claim that a particular Church has the authority to ordain women could be mounted in one of two ways. Either one would have to argue that an all-male ministry was necessary to salvation, that it was a part of the gospel, that it belonged to (in Hooker's terminology) the foundation of faith, or, to put it in terms of modern theology, that it was of the essence of Christianity. But this would imply that those churches — Reformed, Methodist, Baptist, Anglican — which had ordained women had thereby departed from the gospel! So far as I know, no one is claiming this explicitly.

Alternatively, one would have to show that an all-male ministry is (as Hooker put it) a mutable God-given positive law of the Church, that is to say that Christ had ordained it, though without intending it to bind the Church in perpetuity. For as Hooker points out, even some God-given laws of the Church's life are limited according to the purpose and the circumstances in which they are applied. Not all God-given laws are binding on the Church for evermore — as those concerned with baptism and the eucharist are. The fact that they have been universally observed from the beginning is not decisive, for the Church has authority to alter even the laws of the apostles if, there being no command to the contrary, they seem no longer applicable (VII.v.8: 3, p. 162). Then, indeed, as Hooker says, only 'the whole body of the Church', 'by universal consent' would have the power to make a change (VII.v.8: 3, pp. 164f.).

Personally, I do not think that there is any convincing evidence that Jesus did intend an all-male ministry to be a positive law of the Church. But if it were held that he did, then it would follow that only the whole Church would be able to abrogate that law. However, it is significant that neither Rome nor the Orthodox are taking this line. For Rome is now insisting that even the whole Church does not have the authority to do this. In Hooker's terms this means that Rome is placing the all-male ministry on the same level as the dominical sacraments of baptism and the eucharist. Thus, in effect Rome is making an all-male ministry of the essence of Christianity. But it is doing so, not on the basis of a clear dominical or apostolic mandate, but principally on grounds of the unanimity of tradition. For Anglicans, committed to the appeal to scripture and reason, that cannot be decisive. And so I conclude that none of the objections considered invalidates my argument that a branch of the Church has the authority to reform its ministry by admitting women to holy orders.

6

Ministries
in communion?

Contemporary ecumenical theology, as we have seen, is engaged in restructuring the doctrine of the Church in the light of the New Testament concept of *koinonia*. This process must inevitably carry with it important consequences for our understanding of the Church's ministry. However, an analysis of recent agreed statements and other modern ecclesiological texts suggests that these implications have not yet been fully appreciated. There is agreement that *koinonia* carries with it a recovery of the New Testament concept of the corporate priesthood of all Christians. The Second Vatican Council and recent ecumenical dialogue have begun to take this doctrine seriously. But in my judgement they have failed to integrate it with their doctrines of a distinct ordained, set apart ministry within the Church. Indeed, in modern ecclesiology we have not yet succeeded in overcoming the dualism in the doctrine of the ministry that we have inherited from the catholic tradition — a dualism between the priestly 'character' of every baptized Christian, on the one hand, and the priestly role of the ordained ministry, on the other.

It seems clear to me that this dualism will only be overcome when we see that the ordained ministry derives, not from Christ apart from his Church, as though the ministry were autonomous and self-perpetuating, nor from Christ through a clerical succession, which is a patriarchal and hierarchical notion out of place in our modern egalitarian and androgynous society, but from Christ-in-his-body, Christ in the form of the Church, Christ in his whole priestly and apostolic people. There is no access to Christ and his authority and commission except through his body. And this must be so if the ordained ministry is an extension, as it were, of the foundation sacrament of baptism whereby we are incorporated into Christ's threefold office as prophet, priest and king. Understood in this light, the ministerial priesthood becomes the effective symbol of the Church's self-realization — the instrument of the Church's continual discovery and expression of its true nature as a royal priesthood, declaring the wonderful deeds of him who has called it out of darkness into his marvellous light and has constituted it a people for his own possession (1 Peter 2.9–10).

A theology of communion overcomes the old dualism of clergy and laity

Dietrich Bonhoeffer suggested in his youthful study *Communio Sanctorum* that the New Testament has two different concepts of the Church; that of Jerusalem and that of Paul. On the first view, the Jewish-Christian ecclesiology, there was, he wrote (citing Karl Holl), 'from the beginning a proper hierarchy, a divinely established order, a divine church law, a church as an institution, into which the individuals were taken up. A clearly defined group, the "apostles", that is James and the Twelve, possessed a lasting divine pre-eminence, unattainable by any others, and were therefore marked out for the leadership.' This was the basis of the Roman Catholic ecclesiology. But, asserted Bonhoeffer, Paul overcame this view of the Church on the basis of his understanding of the gospel, and Paul's ecclesiology was the source of the Lutheran doctrine of the Church (pp. 97ff.).

That may be a youthful oversimplification on the part of Bonhoeffer (he was only 21 when he published *Communio Sanctorum*) — stereotyping ecclesiologies that were much more dynamic, pragmatic and volatile than this crude juxtaposition suggests. But it may serve to outline a tension that has persisted in ecclesiology through the centuries and still marks our latest ecumenical efforts. It is the tension amounting to dualism between a concept of an authoritative ministry, set apart from the main body of the Church to rule over it and perform priestly functions on its behalf, and a concept of the whole Church as priestly and apostolic and which puts forth instruments or organs of its priestly and apostolic life to service that corporate life.

There can be little doubt that the New Testament celebration of the people of God as a kingdom of priests offering spiritual and living sacrifices to God through Christ, was soon lost sight of and that a priestly caste emerged, distinguishing itself from the body of the Church by appealing to the Old Testament precedent of priests and Levites. By the time of Cyprian in the mid-second century, 'Church and ministry have been distinguished and separated. The ministry now claims a direct descent from the apostles, not *via* the Church, but *via* itself only' (A. T. Hanson, p. 118; R. F. Evans, ch. 2). Cardinal Hume has recently admitted that until the Second Vatican Council the dominant ecclesiology or way of conceiving the Church in his tradition was structural and institutional, 'largely in terms of the perfect society, visible, hierarchical, juridical'. The image was that of a pyramid, 'ascending from the broad base of non-ordained laity, through various layers of hierarchical structure, reaching its apex in the Pope from whom flowed downwards all authority, teaching, ministry and mission'. The corollary of this model was that the laity were regarded (even by themselves) as second-class citizens of God's kingdom — 'a passive supporting cast called on stage when needed by the hierarchy, who are, and always remain the principal protagonists in the mission of the Church' (pp. 66f.). This *societas inaequalis hierarchica* is summed up in the dictum of the great early nineteenth-century dogmatician J. A. Möhler: 'God created the hierarchy and in this way provided amply for everything that was required until the end of time' (Congar, 2, p. 151).

The Roman Catholic Church now wants to embrace the 'more excellent way' of an ecclesiology structured by the concept of *koinonia*. As we have already seen, the Second Vatican Council insisted that all the baptized are united to Christ and participate in his threefold office of ·prophet, priest and king. The Council acknowledged that this conveyed certain privileges and imposed certain duties upon the laity, particularly active participation in the liturgy and in the apostolic mission (apostolate) of the Church.

> Mother Church earnestly desires that all the faithful be led to that full, conscious and active participation in liturgical celebrations which is demanded by the very nature of the liturgy. Such participation by Christian people as 'a chosen race, a royal priesthood, a holy nation, a purchased people' (1 Peter 2.9) is their right and duty by reason of their baptism. (Hume, p. 38)

The Council document on the Lay Apostolate insisted that the laity 'have their own role to play in the mission of the whole people of God in the Church and in the world' and that 'incorporated into Christ's mystical Body through baptism and strengthened by the power of the Holy Spirit through confirmation, they are assigned to the apostolate by the Lord himself' (Hume, pp. 37f.). The new code of canon law reiterated that 'the laity, like all the Christian faithful, are deputed by God to the apostolate through their baptism and confirmation' and should play their part in the furtherance of the gospel throughout the world. When needed, lay people may also give the ministry of the word, lead liturgical prayers, baptize and distribute holy communion (Hume, pp. 50f.).

Cardinal Hume has articulated clearly for us the consequences of a theology of *koinonia* for our understanding of the role of the ordained ministry:

> The bishop and the priest who represents him at parish level is no longer seen at the lonely but all-powerful pinnacle of a pyramid but is the heart of a community, exercising a ministry of word and sacrament, the symbol and source of that unity and communion of faith and love which is the local church. . . . No longer is it appropriate for the priestly ministry to be exercised in splendid isolation and with a semblance of sanctified autocracy. The sharing of the whole people of God in Christ's mission and ministry calls for consultation, collaboration and sharing. (p. 56)

It would be nice to think that it was simply deeper study of the New Testament that had led the Churches to a more authentic understanding of ministry in the context of communion. Alas, it is obvious that social, economic and political realities have also played their part. For the hierarchical, juridical and authoritarian concept of the Church, now disclaimed with such enthusiasm, is only workable where the Church has a monopoly of religious commitment, enforced by legal penalties or supernatural sanctions. Where those legal penalties are abrogated in a secular state and at the same time supernatural sanctions are no longer feared as they were, the hierarchy finds itself presiding over a dwindling power base, one that cannot sustain it financially. Appeal must then be made to the better nature of the rank and file and inducements in the form of spiritual privileges must be offered to them. When pulling rank with the faithful is ineffective, then the call goes out, 'Brothers [perhaps eventually 'sisters', too], we are all in this together. We need one another!' The *societas perfecta* with God-given power to exercise discipline over its members is unworkable in a voluntaristic situation where individuals choose their faith and decide for themselves the extent of their commitment. However, the Roman Catholic Church is not unique in being implicated in unacknowledged social, political and economic forces. The sixteenth-century Reformation in the cities and nation-states of Europe and the rise and fall of the divine right of kings in Anglican ecclesiology are also cases in point. But only when we see the Churches acknowledging their past ideological commitments and the ideological motivation of doctrine and practice will we know that the Spirit of truth is abroad in the Church.

The contemporary theology of communion is struggling to find a way of affirming the priestly vocation of all the baptized without undermining the authority of the ordained ministry. Both the ordained and those they serve need to know that they (the ordained) are ministering *in persona Christi*. It is Christ who baptizes me; Christ who gives me his body and blood under the form of bread and wine; Christ who 'speaks to my heart in the ministry of the word, and Christ whose absolution and blessing send me on my way rejoicing in his peace and presence.

It is just such a concern that has led a Reformed theologian, T. F. Torrance, to insist that the Church's ministry moves from above downwards, not vice versa. Torrance rightly wants to safeguard the truth, so insisted upon by Calvin, for example, that 'the ministry of the Church is related to the ministry of Christ in such a way that in and through the ministry of the Church it is always Christ himself who is at work, nourishing, sustaining, ordering and governing his Church on earth' (*Royal Priesthood*, p. 37). This leads Torrance to affirm that 'the whole direction of the Church's ministry is determined by a movement from the Head of the Body downward to the members of the Body, from the ascended Lord downward to his Church' (p. 38). The ministry is therefore not a function of the people or of their delegates. It is not democratically grounded. The people do not put forth their representatives before God. As Torrance points out, Paul never speaks of himself as the representative of the Church before God or as acting on its behalf towards God, and certainly not as responsible or answerable to the Church for what he does on its behalf (p. 40).

I must confess that I find this an over-dualistic conception of the relation between Christ and the Church, and therefore between the Church and its ministry, and I wonder whether the later Torrance, who has been vigorously combating dualism in all its forms, would remain satisfied with it. I also think that the New Testament, as the late John Robinson taught us in his book *The Body*, has a much more realist understanding of the Church as the body of Christ. True, it sometimes speaks of the Church's Head in heaven and his body on earth but it also speaks of the whole Christ residing embodied in his Church.

Only a more integrated, almost holistic, conception of the relation between the universal and the ministerial priesthood can do justice to the New Testament picture of the Church. As we shall now see, recent ecumenical ecclesiology has not achieved that integrated conception.

There is an ecumenical consensus on the relation of the ministerial and universal priesthoods but it deserves to be challenged

Recent ecumenical theology has spoken with one voice about the relation between the universal priesthood of baptized Christians and the priesthood of the ordained ministry. A number of 'agreed statements' define these as two distinct ways in which the Church participates in the priesthood of Christ. They envisage his priesthood as being mediated to the Church through parallel channels: the priesthood of all the baptized on the one hand and the ordained ministerial priesthood on the other. They are strikingly insistent that the ministerial priesthood is not derived from or delegated by the universal priesthood. Is this a wonderful example of ecumenical convergence and consensus, perhaps attributable to the hand of divine providence? Has 'the mind of the Church' spoken? Has the *consensus fidelium* become a reality? Or have our ecclesiologists, for whatever reason, corporately embraced an ultimately incoherent doctrine? Let us trace its pedigree.

The Second Vatican Council   The notion of the priesthood of Christ being mediated to the Church through the parallel channels of the universal and ministerial priesthood derives, in its modern expression, from the Second Vatican Council's Dogmatic Constitution on the Church *Lumen Gentium* (1964). The Council unequivocally affirmed that all the baptized are incorporated into Christ and participate in his priesthood. 'The baptized, by regeneration and the anointing of the Holy Spirit, are consecrated into a spiritual house and a holy priesthood . . . they can offer spiritual sacrifices.' Regarding the laity, we read: 'These faithful are by baptism made one body with Christ and are established among the people of God. They are in their own way made sharers in the priestly, prophetic and kingly functions of Christ.' However, when we ask how this universal priesthood, so evangelically affirmed by Vatican II, relates to the ordained priesthood, we receive the following answer:

> Though they differ from one another in essence and not only in degree, the common priesthood of the faithful and the ministerial or hierarchical priesthood are none the less interrelated. Each of them in its own special way is a participation in the one priesthood of Christ. (V2, pp. 27, 57)

As Edmund Hill has recently commented, this is one of the less satisfactory statements of Vatican II in that it fails to explain how these two manifestations of Christ's priesthood are related or how they differ in their mode of participating in that priesthood. There are several reasons why the Council was unable to pursue this question to a satisfactory conclusion. As Edmund Hill suggests, 'a Catholic theology of the common priesthood had been so little developed, and a theology of the ministerial priesthood has been so overdeveloped in a wrong direction' (p. 128). A deeper historical reason is that the Second Vatican Council saw the confrontation of two ecclesiologies — that of Vatican I, the juridical, canonical, hierarchical approach symbolized by the decree on papal infallibility *Pastor aeternus* (1870), and that of the developing theology of the Church as a communion which was ultimately dominant. But, as Tillard has put it, 'the ecclesiology of Vatican II is not perfectly unified. In spite of preference accorded to one ecclesiology over the other, we hear in Vatican II, and even in *Lumen Gentium*, a distinct jarring produced by clumsy lack of co-ordination between the ecclesiologies' ('The Church of God is a Communion', p. 117). Finally, the concept of individual Christians participating to different degrees (or as modern statements tactfully prefer, in different ways) in the priesthood of Christ, finds its classical conceptualization in the notion of 'character' as defined and refined by St Thomas Aquinas and makes little sense without it. This concept will concern us shortly.

Post-Vatican II official Roman Catholic teaching The dualism of *Lumen Gentium*, between the ordained and the universal priesthood, was perpetuated in the document of the Synod of Bishops 1967 on the ministerial priesthood (*Ultimis temporibus*), which declared the 'priestly ministry' to be 'distinct from the common priesthood of all the faithful', 'in essence and not merely in degree' (Flannery, p. 679).

Pope John Paul II, while affirming emphatically that all the faithful share in Christ's offices of prophet, priest and king, has operated a distinction between participating in those offices in a *baptismal* manner, as the faithful do, and in a *hierarchical* manner, as do the ordained, whose role is to 'activate' the prophetic, priestly and kingly role of the faithful. Deacons activate only the kingly office, priests the kingly and the priestly, and bishops the kingly, priestly and prophetic offices (Hogan and Le Voir, pp. 123ff.).

The hierarchical concept of ordination no doubt underlies the present Pope's opposition to the ordination of women. For St Thomas Aquinas, the sacrament of order could not be imparted to a woman because her subordinate position as helpmeet for the male carried with it an inherent inability to signify the hierarchical excellence of the priesthood or to receive power. As Aquinas puts it: 'the female sex cannot signify any superiority of rank, for woman is in a state of subjection' (*ST*, Supp. 39.1.c; cf. Børresen, p. 237).

The Anglican–Roman Catholic International Commission   The first agreed statement to adopt Vatican II's approach was the Canterbury statement on Ministry and Ordination (1973) of the Anglican–Roman Catholic International Commission (ARCIC I). According to this report, ordained ministers of the Church have a twofold relation to the Christian community. On the one hand, 'they share through baptism in the priesthood of the people of God'. On the other, they are — particularly when presiding at the eucharist — 'representative of the whole church in the fulfilment of its priestly vocation of self-offering to God as a living sacrifice'. But what is the connection between the two? 'Nevertheless', the commission continues, 'their ministry is not an extension of the common Christian priesthood but belongs to another realm of the gifts of the Spirit.' The *Elucidation* (1979) of the statement on Ministry and Ordination adds that the priesthood of the people of God and of the ordained ministry 'are two distinct realities which relate, each in its own way, to the high priesthood of Christ, the unique priesthood of the new covenant, which is their source and model' (*FR*, pp. 36, 41).

The Roman Catholic–Lutheran Joint Commission   The report *The Ministry in the Church* (1981) emphasized the dominical institution and divine authority of the ordained ministry. It 'makes present the mission of Jesus Christ'. The report goes on: 'The presence of this ministry in the community "signifies the priority of divine initiative and authority in the church's existence". Consequently, this ministry is not simply a delegation "from below", but is instituted by Jesus Christ.' In a note, the report refers to the words of the Second Vatican Council but repudiates any notion of laity and clergy participating to different degrees in Christ's priesthood:

> When Vatican II affirms that the ordained ministry differs from the common priesthood of all the baptized in essence and not in degree . . . this [present] formulation wants to say the following: the church's ministry cannot be derived from the congregation, but it is also not an enhancement of the common priesthood, and the minister as such is not a Christian to a greater degree. The ministry is rather situated on a different level; it includes the ministerial priesthood which is interrelated with the common priesthood. (*Growth in Agreement*, pp. 253ff.)

Whether this Roman Catholic–Lutheran report gains anything by substituting 'levels' for 'degrees' may be doubted.

The World Council of Churches Lima Statement   The so-called Lima statement of 1982, *Baptism, Eucharist, Ministry* (*BEM*), achieved a remarkable degree of consensus, but this was sometimes attained by giving a wide berth to contentious issues. Soundly insisting that 'the ordained ministry has no existence apart from the community', the statement goes on to delineate the relation between Christ, the Church and the ordained ministry in very general and non-contentious terms. 'Ordained ministers are related, as are all Christians, both to the priesthood of Christ, and to the priesthood of the church' (*BEM*, pp. 22f.). By confining its elucidation of the relation between the universal and the ministerial priesthood to the word 'related', *BEM* refrains from endorsing Vatican II's notion of parallel mediations of the priesthood of Christ to the Church, at the price of failing to advance theological understanding on this particular point.

Anglican–Reformed dialogue   The report *God's Reign and Our Unity* (1984), produced by representatives of the Anglican Communion and of the worldwide Reformed tradition, bears a not unequivocal relation to the teaching of Vatican II and the emerging consensus of ecumenical theology on the question of the relation between the universal and the ministerial priesthood. The commission agrees that ordained ministers may legitimately be called priests. It goes on: 'They exercise their priestly ministry neither apart from the priesthood of the whole body, nor by derivation from the priesthood of the whole body, but by virtue of their participation, in company with the whole body, in the priestly ministry of the risen Christ' (p. 51). Here the commission seems to line up with the Vatican II concept of parallel mediations of Christ's priesthood. The Church of England report *The Priesthood of the Ordained Ministry* (which we will turn to next) certainly takes it in this sense and claims its support. I must confess that I find the above statement with its 'neither apart from . . . nor by derivation from . . . but by virtue of . . . in company with' somewhat tortuous, elusive and unconvincing.

However, the report seems to recover its equilibrium when it returns to its shared Reformation heritage, and what follows clearly distances this statement from the Vatican II orthodoxy in this matter. 'The one who presides does so, not in virtue of a different relationship to the life of the risen Christ from the rest of the body, but because — as a matter of order — he has been so authorized.' In a context stressing the representative function of the minister, the report reiterates:

> The presidency of the ordained person does not depend upon his possessing a priesthood which others lack; it depends upon the good ordering which is essential to the life of the church as it exercises corporately the priesthood given to it by the one who is alone the good [*sic*] High Priest. (pp. 52f.)

This concept of order, or as one might say, of economy, is opposed to all talk of 'essence' and all dualism of lay and clerical modes of participating in Christ's priesthood.

The Priesthood of the Ordained Ministry (1986)   This report of the Church of England's Faith and Order Advisory Group (FOAG) is the latest document to recycle the notion of the priesthood of Christ being mediated to the Church through parallel but distinct channels — the universal priesthood of the baptized on the one hand, and the ordained ministerial priesthood on the other. Though not itself an ecumenical agreed statement, it refers to several such agreements in its support and also to *Lumen Gentium*.

> The common priesthood of the community and the special priesthood of the ordained ministry are both derived from the priesthood of Christ. Bishops and presbyters do not participate to a greater degree in the priesthood of Christ; they participate in a different way — not that is as individual believers, but in the exercise of their office. Thus theirs is not a magnified form of the common priesthood; the difference is this, that their ministry is an appointed means through which Christ makes his priesthood present and effective to his people. (pp. 99f.)

In tune with its sources, FOAG insists that the authority of the ordained ministry is 'not simply delegated to it by the community. . . . Its priesthood is not simply derived from the priestliness of the whole community. . . . It has a particular relationship to Christ, which is not simply derived from the common ministry of all Christians.' I must confess that I find that repeated use of 'simply' tendentious! 'The lady doth protest too much, methinks.'

This then is the received wisdom of modern ecumenical theology. A consensus has established itself. Anyone challenging it would seem to be a voice in the wilderness. But is this an ecumenical breakthrough, or a case of the uncritical borrowing of dubious theology because it seems to provide a plausible form of words? In what follows I aim to show that this ecumenical consensus is incompatible with significant elements in all the major Christian traditions.

The doctrine of two parallel and distinct channels of the mediation of Christ's priesthood to the church is inconsistent with the Roman Catholic, the Anglican and the Reformation traditions

The Roman Catholic tradition The idea that lay and ordained Christians participate in different ways in the priesthood of Christ was classically formulated by St Thomas Aquinas in terms of sacramental 'character'. For Aquinas, 'character is a certain kind of seal by which the soul is marked off' for an appropriate degree of participation in divine worship and ministry. Character is thus a sort of (the vagueness is unavoidable) mark of consecration setting the believer apart in order that he or she may both receive and hand on the means of grace. Sacramental character is the character of Christ as priest. Through the unrepeatable sacraments of baptism, confirmation and ordination Christians participate in Christ's priesthood through being conformed (or configured) to that priesthood to a varying extent according to whether the character received is that belonging to baptism, confirmation or orders:

> Sacramental character consists in a certain participation in Christ's priesthood present in the faithful. It is present in the sense that just as Christ has the full power of a spiritual priesthood, so his faithful are brought into configuration to him in that they share in a certain spiritual power relating to the sacraments and things pertaining to divine worship.

Aquinas has here developed what was in St Augustine little more than a metaphor derived from the marking or branding of soldiers into a philosophical concept. Though it remains somewhat elusive and enigmatic, Aquinas warns against taking it in any ontological sense when he states that character resides in the powers, not the essence, of the soul (*ST*, IIIa, q. 63, articles 3, 4, 5). The concept of sacramental character was reinforced by the Councils of Florence (1439; DS 1313) and Trent, particularly in condemnation of Luther's functional notion of ordination (DS 1609, 1767, 1774).

Vatican II was not keen to deploy the concept of sacramental character, making extremely limited use of it in *Lumen Gentium* (21; V2, p. 42) and in the dogmatic constitution on the priesthood (2; V2, p. 535). Naturally, it would be quite incongruous in ecumenical agreed statements. But as these statements clutched at one of the least satisfactory pieces of Vatican II definition, the concept of character (which provided the original rationale for the conceptual scheme in which different orders in the Church participated to varying degrees in Christ's priesthood) was quietly dropped. But without it, the doctrine espoused by successive ecumenical commissions remains incoherent.

The Anglican tradition It is surprising that Anglicans engaged in ecumenical dialogue have not made greater use of their doctrine of the representative nature of the ministerial priesthood. Where they have, they have not always appreciated the intrinsic logic of this doctrine. A succession of Anglican theologians — F. D. Maurice, J. B. Lightfoot, Charles Gore and R. C. Moberly — developed this concept during the second half of the nineteenth century (see Avis, *Anglicanism*, pp. 167ff.). As the mouthpiece or delegate of a priestly people, the priest represented them before God, and they acted through him. Let Gore, whose 'catholic' credentials are surely impeccable, speak for this tradition. For Gore, the priest is the representative of the whole body of the Church which is itself priestly, first, because it lives in the full enjoyment of Christ's reconciliation of us to the Father, and, second, because it is the instrument through which God chooses to reconcile the world to himself. Within this priestly body there are, it is true, those who are especially entrusted and commissioned with the ministry of reconciliation, but theirs — Gore is quite explicit — is a difference of *function* not of kind (p. 84; cf. Avis, *Gore*, p. 37). Anyone who had attended seriously to this fine exposition of the doctrine of a priesthood that is representative of God to humanity and humanity to God could hardly have been so dismissive of the suggestion that the ordained ministry is derived from the common priesthood of all Christians.

It is gratifying to find that the 1988 Lambeth Conference does not employ the two-source theology of ministry of much recent ecumenical ecclesiology. The 'Mission and Ministry' report is admirably clear that 'our baptism carries with it the implied gift of authority for ministry' and 'the foundation of all ministry is that royal priesthood of all God's people with which, by virtue of his or her baptism, every Christian is called to exercise a ministry . . .' (L88, pp. 51, 54).

The Reformation tradition For Aquinas, as we have seen, there appear to be different degrees of participation in Christ's priesthood — the sacrament of order conveying a greater participation than the sacraments of baptism or confirmation, because baptism does not qualify the individual to minister the means of grace to others (except baptism in an emergency) but simply to receive them for him- or herself. For Luther, on the other hand, there can be no degrees of participation in the priesthood of the Christ to whom all believers are equally and fully united by baptism. Neither can there be different *modes* of sharing in that priesthood for clergy and laity.

It is a striking fact that Luther's early popular polemical writings laid more stress on the doctrine of the universal priesthood than on the tenet of justification by faith. The universal priesthood was at the heart of Luther's reform. It is not an appendage to evangelical theology but simply a paraphrase of the Reformation concept of the Church.

All Christians are priests by virtue of the gospel and baptism. If we have Christ's gospel, we have Christ himself and all that is his. 'Now he who has faith and is a Christian also has Christ; now if he has Christ, so that everything Christ has is his, he also has the power to forgive sins; and if a Christian has the power to forgive sins, he also has the power to do everything a priest can do.' Entrusted thus with the gospel, the believer must offer it wherever it is needed, especially in bringing comfort to distressed consciences. What is the difference, Luther demands, between preaching the gospel and saying 'Thy sins are forgiven thee'? (*WA*, 10 III, pp. 394f.).

In baptism every Christian is consecrated priest. Baptism invalidates the division between clergy and laity and, in terms of medieval society, between the spiritual and the temporal estates. 'All Christians are truly of the spiritual estate and there is no difference among them except that of office . . . we are all consecrated priests through baptism' (*LW*, 44, p. 127).

This power of priesthood in which all Christians share equally includes, first, the right to administer the sacraments of baptism and the eucharist (*WA*, 6, p. 566; 15, p. 720) and second, the authority to judge doctrinal questions (*WA*, 15, p. 720) and the right and duty to teach the faith (*WA*, 8, p. 423). Luther supports this aspect of the universal priesthood by reference to a parent's responsibility to teach the children (*WA*, 17 I, p. 509), just as he supports the right to administer the sacrament from the common practice of midwives baptizing infants in an emergency (*LW*, 40, p. 23). Third, it includes the exercise of the keys, the absolving of penitent souls, which Luther regards simply as one particular application of the gospel (*LW*, 3, p. 124; 40, pp. 27f.). Finally, the priesthood is an office of intercession before God for others. 'To appear before God on behalf of others' is the key phrase in Luther's statements of the universal priesthood (*coram deo apparere pro aliis orare; für Gott treten, eyner für den andern bitte: WA*, 7, p. 54; 12, p. 307). The pastoral character of the universal priesthood is supreme.

Any Christian can represent Christ to administer spiritual counsel to a brother or sister. All Christians are permitted 'most freely to hear the confession of secret sins, so that the sinner may make his sins known to whomever he will and seek pardon and comfort, that is, the word of Christ, by the mouth of his neighbour' (*LW*, 36, p. 88). Luther recommends that you go first to the priest — but 'only because he is a brother and a Christian' (*WA*, 8, p. 184). The office of priesthood which is every Christian's birthright is thus one of mutual service, counsel and comfort in which the gospel is shared among Christians according to their various needs and troubles.

However, Luther's teaching on the universal priesthood is not the recipe for anarchy in the Church that it seems. The controlling factor was the call of the Church. Luther lays down the principle that what is common to all (the priesthood), no individual may presume to take upon himself without the consent of all. Though all have the same power, he says in *The Babylonian Captivity of the Church*, 'no one may make use of this power except by the consent of the community or by the call of a superior. For what is the common property of all no individual may arrogate to himself unless he is called' (*LW*, 32, p. 116). And in the *Appeal to the Christian Nobility* he writes: 'Because we are all priests of equal standing, no one must push himself forward and take it upon himself without our consent and election, to do that for which we all have equal authority. For no one dare take upon himself what is common to all without the authority and consent of the community' (*LW*, 44, p. 129).

It follows that, for Luther, ordination bestows not priesthood but the authority to exercise a ministry on behalf of the whole body. It is merely an ecclesiastical ceremony (*ritus ecclesiasticus*) that ratifies the call and election of a minister. Obviously no indelible character is bestowed: public ministry is merely a function that the designated individual exercises for the time being. He may give up his office or be deposed, becoming a layman again.

> Should it happen that a person chosen for such office were deposed for lack of trust, he would then be exactly what he was before. Therefore a priest in Christendom is nothing else but an office-holder. As long as he holds office he takes precedence; where he is deposed he is a peasant or a townsman like anybody else! (*LW*, 44, p. 129)

Although Luther held that women could not exercise public office (cf. Avis, *Church in the Reformers*, pp. 106f.), they share equally in the royal priesthood that Christ imparts to his people. The common practice of midwives administering baptism is proof of this: 'When women baptise, they exercise the function of priesthood legitimately and do it not as a private act but as a part of the public ministry of the church' (*LW*, 40, p. 23). Thus administered, the sacrament of baptism is a fully effective means of grace in which 'sin is taken away, eternal death abolished, the prince of the world cast out, heaven bestowed; in short, by which the divine majesty pours itself forth through all the soul' (*LW*, 40, p. 25). When Luther grants women the power to baptize, he recognizes that this carries with it all the other priestly functions, for the sacrament of baptism includes the ministry of the word and is, in Luther's view, the highest of all priestly functions.

Thus, for Luther, every baptized Christian enjoys the fullness of Christ's priesthood. As he provocatively puts it: 'Whoever comes out of the water of baptism can boast that he is already a consecrated priest, bishop and pope' (*LW*, 36, p. 116). A Christian needs no further bestowal of sacramental 'character' if he is called to exercise a ministry on behalf of the whole priestly body, but he must be called and authorized for this ministry.

The Orthodox tradition The teaching of the Orthodox tradition about the relation between the universal priesthood of the faithful and the sacramental priesthood of the clergy cannot be read off from the pronouncements of a central magisterium, as in the case of Rome, for no such magisterium exists in Orthodoxy. But as with Anglicanism, the consensus of the tradition must be derived from its recognized theologians. However, my limited acquaintance with Orthodox theologians has not revealed a unanimous view on this question, but rather a tension. This in itself is interesting, as the Orthodox lay great store by the supposed unanimity of their tradition.

On the one hand, we have a strand of the tradition that makes a clear dichotomy between the universal and the ministerial priesthood. For example, the ancient Syriac tradition distinguished between the priesthood of all the baptized, which depended on growth in holiness and was exercised towards the world outside the Church, and the ministerial priesthood of the clergy, which was not dependent on growth in holiness, and was exercised towards the community within the Church (Brock).

For Methodios Fouyas the Roman and Orthodox Churches are agreed on this question. They both recognize two kinds of priesthood: spiritual and sacramental.

> The priesthood to which special members are sacramentally ordained in the Church, is that which Christ committed to his Apostles and which is continued down into our day by the Apostolic succession. All who are baptized hold the spiritual priesthood, enabling them to be in union with the ordained priest and to participate in the liturgical worship in which they offer the holy oblation.

Fouyas endorses the teaching of Pope Pius XII in *Mediator Dei*, that only the priest represents Jesus Christ and the people 'in no sense represent the Divine Redeemer', as correspondingly 'absolutely to Orthodox teaching' (Fouyas, pp. 194f.). (This dualism of clergy and laity has been undermined in the post-Vatican II teaching of the Roman Catholic Church about the apostolate of the laity: of course the laity represent Christ, that is their *raison d'être* in the Church and the world!)

Furthermore, Kallistos Ware has written about the relation between the ministerial and the universal priesthood in terms that correspond closely to the current ecumenical consensus that stems from certain inchoate remarks of Vatican II.

> The ministerial priest is not to be seen in secular and pseudo-democratic terms, as a deputy or representative merely exercising by delegation the royal priesthood that belongs to Christian people as a whole. On the contrary, the ministerial priest derives his priesthood not by delegation from the people, but immediately from Christ. . . . The royal priesthood and the ministerial priesthood are both ways of sharing *directly* in the priesthood of Christ, and neither is derived by devolution through the other. (Hopko (ed.), pp. 22f.)

On the other hand, however, a different strand of teaching about the relation between the universal and the ministerial priesthood is apparent in some recent Orthodox writing. This finds support in the Moscow agreed statement of the Anglican–Orthodox dialogue (1976) which stated:

> In the Eucharist the eternal priesthood of Christ is constantly manifested in time. The celebrant, in his liturgical action, has a twofold ministry: as an icon of Christ, acting in the name of Christ, towards the community and also *as a representative of the community expressing the priesthood of the faithful.* (p. 89; my emphasis)

A clearly functional distinction between the universal and ministerial priesthoods has been developed by O. Clément in his article significantly entitled 'Orthodox ecclesiology as an ecclesiology of Communion'. In Clément's understanding, all Christians, including members of the hierarchy, constitute the *laos*, the priestly people of God, and are endowed with the Spirit through baptism–chrismation and the eucharist. Chrism — an inseparable part of baptism for the Orthodox — is 'the sacrament of the universal priesthood'.

> Everyone who is baptized and sealed by the Spirit is king, priest and prophet within the one *laos theou*. Baptism–chrismation and the Eucharist endow all the members of the Church with exactly the same priestly quality, through the working of the same sanctifying grace which alone has an ontological effect. (p. 116)

In the Body of Christ everyone is both layperson and priest. Clément cites Paul Evdokimov's assertion that the distinction between the universal and the ministerial priesthoods 'is functional and brings about no ontological difference' (Clément, pp. 116f.).

Orthodoxy, in contrast to Rome, has also emphasized the kingly and prophetic roles of all Christians. As sharers in Christ's kingly office, the 'laity' govern the parish under the chairmanship of the priest and take part in synods. As sharers in Christ's prophetic office, they serve as teachers, catechists and theologians, though doctrine is always ultimately articulated by the bishops corporately. Orthodox theologians are often lay people: Cabasilas, Khomyakov, Lossky and Evdokimov are shining examples.

Finally, Zizioulas has attempted to transcend the distinction of ontology versus function in our interpretation of the ministry by presenting the ministry as *identical* both with the ministry of Christ himself and with the ministry of the community. First, there is no ministry in the Church other than the ministry of Christ. 'The Church's ministry realizes here and now the very saving work of Christ, which involves *the very personal life* and presence of the one who saves' (*Being*, pp. 211f.). Second, there is no ministry in the Church other than the ministry of the community. The ministry of any priest cut off from the community is dead, because the ordained individual becomes a 'relational entity', a true 'person'. Therefore the question whether ordination is ontological or functional is not merely misleading but impossible.

> In the light of the *koinonia* of the Holy Spirit, ordination relates the ordained man so profoundly and so existentially to the community that in his new state after ordination he cannot be any longer, as a minister, conceived in himself. In this state, existence is determined by *communion* which qualifies and defines both 'ontology' and 'function'. (pp. 226f.)

The ordained priest is engaged in 'representation by participation' (p. 230).

While Zizioulas' distinctive idiom cannot be directly translated into the vocabulary of Western ecclesiology, it is abundantly clear that his holistic, identitarian approach can only disdain the dualism implied in the ecumenical consensus which postulates two parallel channels of the mediation of Christ's priesthood to the Church.

Fullness of priesthood resides within the whole priestly body of the Church

The concept of two parallel lines of transmission of Christ's priesthood to the Church — through the universal priesthood of the baptized, on the one hand, and through the ordained ministerial priesthood on the other, which recent ecumenical theology has found so serviceable, fails to overcome the inherited dualism of clergy and laity. It places these two manifestations of priesthood side by side unintegrated. But it also adds to the old dualism a new dualism: it presupposes and perpetuates a false dichotomy between the ascended Christ and his body the Church. It treats the image of the Church as the body of Christ as a mere metaphor. It does not fully reckon with the New Testament's emphasis on Christ dwelling embodied (*somatikos*) in the Church. A more realist approach would affirm that while Christ is, of course, the ultimate source of the ordained ministerial priesthood, the proximate source of this priesthood is the Church in its corporate existence as communion (*koinonia*). For the ordained ministry is a function, organ and instrument of the life of the whole priestly body that is united to Christ through baptism and now lives in the enjoyment of his priestly office. This makes the ordained ministry an *economy* internal to the life of the Church.

How else does the ordained ministry receive Christ's authority if not through the Church? A tactile apostolic succession that by-passes *koinonia* is out of keeping with an ecumenical theology of communion. In any case, it would be a strange notion for Lutheran and Reformed Churches to embrace. Yet, as we have seen, in recent agreed statements they seem to have left themselves open to this interpretation by toying with the notion of two parallel sources of the mediation of Christ's priesthood to the Church. Even within the Anglican tradition, insistence on apostolic succession as the exclusive source of ministerial authority (unchurching non-episcopal communions as a result) was an aberration brought about by reaction to the failure of the divinely appointed royal supremacy in church government (see Avis, *Anglicanism*). Where else does the fullness of Christ's priesthood reside if not in the body of the Church?

The whole Church receives the fullness of Christ   The Church is 'his body, the fullness of him who fills all in all' (Ephesians 1.22f.). Though the translation of this text is uncertain, on any interpretation Christ, who himself receives the fullness (*pleroma*) of the divine life, pours this life into his body the Church, so that the Church enjoys the plenitude of all that is Christ's. Thus the NEB renders: God 'appointed him [Christ] as supreme head to the Church, which is his body and as such holds within it the fullness of him who himself receives the entire fullness of God'. There is no other source — certainly no *higher* source — of Christian priesthood than that messianic body which is continually being corporately filled with the life of God.

As the writer of Colossians puts it: 'For in him the whole fullness (*pleroma*) of deity dwells bodily (*somatikos*), and you have come to fullness of life in him, who is the head of all rule and authority' (2.9f.). A comparison with 1 Corinthians 11.3, 8 suggests (following Barrett's commentary, p. 248 and Bedale) that *kephale* (literally, head) should be rendered origin or source here. Then it almost becomes equivalent to *arche*, beginning, origin, signifying priority and source of existence. A parallelism of *kephale* and *arche* occurs in Colossians 1.18f.: 'He is the head (*kephale*) of the body, the church; he is the beginning (*arche*), the first-born from the dead, that in everything he might be pre-eminent. For in him all the fullness (*pleroma*) of God was pleased to dwell . . .' (cf. Colossians 2.10: *he kephale pases arches*, the head of all principle). Paul is laying it down in 1 Corinthians 11 that 'the head (*kephale*) of every man is Christ, the head of a woman is her husband, and the head of Christ is God' (v. 3). Therefore women, but not men, should cover their heads when praying or prophesying (vv. 4–7), 'for man was not made from woman, but woman from man' (v. 8). Here the sense of origin or source is clear. This interpretation of *kephale* is substantiated in Ephesians 4.13–16 where the writer speaks of Christ ascending far above all the heavens 'that he might fill all things' (v. 10), and giving his gifts of ministry to the Church 'for building up the body of Christ' (v. 12), so that we may attain 'to mature manhood, to the measure of the stature of the fullness of Christ' (v. 13) and 'grow up in every way into him who is the head (*kephale*)' and who is the source of all that the Church requires that it may build itself up in love (vv. 15f.). We might compare Colossians 2.19: 'the Head, from whom the whole body, nourished and knit together . . . grows with a growth that is from God'. It is then as thus embodied that Christ is the source of all ministry in the Church.

As John Robinson wrote in his contribution to *The Historic Episcopate*:

> The ministry is the ministry of Christ only as it is the ministry of the Church. All that is said of the ministry in the New Testament is said not of individuals nor of some apostolic college or 'essential ministry' but of the whole Body. . . . The whole life of Christ is given to the Church to be possessed *in solidum* . . . . Christ's life is now lived and given 'bodywise' (*somatikos*), not individually but corporately, so that the fullness of God now resides in him as it resides at the same time in us his members. (p. 14)

The whole Church shares in Christ's apostolate   The notion that the ordained ministry acts *in persona Christi* is familiar in both Catholic and Protestant theology. Without denying this truth, we have to go further and affirm that the whole Church acts *in persona Christi*, because Christ acts through his Church. Alan Richardson begins his account of the New Testament's theology of ministry thus:

> The ministry of the Church is the continuation of the apostolic and priestly ministry of Christ himself. . . . His ministry to the world is fulfilled through the instrumentality of his resurrection body, the Church. All true ministerial acts of the Church are *gesta Christi*, the acts of Christ, the Head

of the body. Christ is still the one who commissions and sends the pastors of his flock; he is the celebrant at every Eucharist, the minister of every act of loving service that his disciples perform in his name. (p. 291)

Jesus sent his apostles out bearing his personal authority to stand for and represent him. They were his envoys (*šĕlūhîm*) and, according to the rabbis (Berakot 5.5) a man's envoy (*šālîah*) was as himself. (Rengstorf, *TDNT*, 1, pp. 398–447; Barrett, 'Shaliah and Apostle'). Jesus himself was deeply conscious of having been sent by the Father and sent forth his apostles as an extension of his own mission. 'As the Father has sent me, even so I send you' (John 20.21). The shared apostolicity of Christ and his disciples is not confined to John. Matthew has: 'He who receives you receives me, and he who receives me receives him who sent me' (10.40). Apostolic authority has, of course, traditionally been claimed for the ordained ministry and a distinct apostolate has been set over against the ministry of the laity to counterbalance, as it were, the universal priesthood. But what we have to grasp is the radical teaching of the New Testament that the whole Church is apostolic. The whole Church is 'sent'. All Christians share in the apostolate. The apostolate is not, therefore, an order within the Church that can be deployed against the laity when it grows restive!

How can this be justified? Surely in the New Testament it is the twelve apostles who are sent forth with Christ's authority to remit or retain sins, to bind and loose? Yes indeed, but the twelve apostles *were* the Church. They were the Church in nucleus, the faithful remnant through whom the promises of God would be fulfilled. They were the pioneers of a Church that would expand to fill the whole earth (cf. A. T. Hanson). It was F. J. A. Hort who pointed out that if the apostles were not the ecclesia, but simply an order within it, the eucharist could not have been intended for all Christians, for only the twelve were present at the Last Supper (p. 30). It might also be said that if the apostles were not the Church, then the Holy Spirit was not intended for all Christians, for it was upon them that Jesus breathed saying 'Receive the Holy Spirit', according to John 20.22. In this too they were the nucleus, the representative Church, for the Spirit came later upon the whole community, about 120 persons on the day of Pentecost, according to Luke (Acts 1.15; 2.1). This comparison also suggests that the commission — the sending with power to remit or retain sins in John 20.21–23 — is intended for the whole Church. Similarly, in the high priestly prayer of John 17 it is clear that the Lord's intercession for those whom the Father has given him out of the world is not restricted to the twelve but includes all who will believe in him through their word of testimony, for his prayer is that they may all be one as he is one with the Father. It is of all his own that Jesus says: 'As thou didst send me into the world, so I have sent them into the world . . . so that the world may know that thou hast sent me' (vv. 18, 23). As A. T. Hanson puts it: 'The apostolicity of the Church consists in being the Church' (p. 157).

The whole Church is constituted by its priestly nature   It is well known that in the New Testament the set apart ministry of the Church is not designated a priesthood. There are apostles, deacons, presbyters and overseers (*episcopi*) but not priests. The priesthood of the Church is a corporate reality. The only use of the word priesthood (*hierateuma*) is in 1 Peter 2 where all Christians are included. Priest (*hiereus* = Latin *sacerdos*) is used of Christian believers only in Revelation: he 'who loves us and has freed us from our sins by his blood [has] made us a kingdom, priests to his God and Father' (1.5f.); the faithful martyrs who are privileged to rise in the first resurrection are made 'priests of God and of Christ and . . . reign with him for a thousand years' (20.6). In other words there is no hint of a priestly order or priestly caste in the New Testament. On the contrary, all Christians are priests by virtue of their baptism. 'Baptism is, as it were, the ordination of a new member of the royal priesthood' (Richardson, p. 301).

The writer of 1 Peter (2.4–10) employs all the titles of ancient Israel to show that the promises and purposes of God are fulfilled in his Church. The Church is a new Israel ('a chosen race, a holy nation'); a new temple ('a spiritual house'); a new priesthood ('a holy priesthood'); a new royal house or dynasty (following Kelly, p. 96); offering new sacrifices ('spiritual sacrifices'); and uttering prophecy ('that you may declare the wonderful deeds of him'; cf. Acts 2.11: 'telling . . . the mighty works of God'). The baptismal reference in 'called . . . out of darkness into his marvellous light' (v. 9) is clear by comparison with the baptismal imagery of illumination in Romans 13.12, Ephesians 5.14 and Hebrews 6.4 and 10.32 (Kelly, p. 100).

What then are the 'spiritual' and 'living' sacrifices (as opposed to material and immolated animal sacrifices of the Old Testament) that Christians offer to God through Christ as their priestly work? They are: first, themselves ('your bodies': Romans 12.1); second, charity and fellowship (it is significant that *koinonia* is offered sacrificially to God: Hebrews 13.16); third, material support for the apostolic ministry (Philippians 4.18); fourth, praises and prayers (Hebrews 13.15; Revelation 8.3f.; 5.8); and finally, new converts to the Christian gospel, the first fruits of the Gentiles (Romans 15.16; Colossians 1.28; Revelation 14.4f.).

The whole work of Christian life, devotion, and ministry is thus conceived as a sacrificial offering by a priesthood that has come into being through baptism. The Christian life is constituted by its priestly task and therefore the whole Church is constituted in existence by its priestly nature. Where we have the baptized, living in the exercise of their baptismal gift, we have priestly work and there we have the Church. When the priestly community puts forth, as it were, instruments, organs or agents of its priestly character in the form of a set apart, ordained ministry, it is that it might reflect back to the whole Church its priestly status, leading the way in doing what the whole Church itself must do and acting as the whole Church must act.

If we recognize a church's baptism, we must recognize its ministry

The implications of this New Testament theology — of fullness of priesthood dwelling in the whole body of the Church — for ecumenical progress towards mutual recognition of ministries is not far to seek. It can be indicated in a series of fairly logical steps.

First, baptism is the foundational sacrament: all other sacramental acts (penance, holy communion, ministerial order) are appropriations, applications or extensions of the basic baptismal reality.

Second, by baptism we are incorporated into the body of Christ, the Church, and participate in Christ's threefold messianic office as prophet, priest and king.

Third, all Christians exercise their priesthood in a continual offering of spiritual sacrifice to God through Christ.

Fourth, the Church needs to set apart some members of the *laos*, the people of God, to represent and service its own inherent priesthood and to reflect it back, so enhancing the Church's sense of priestly vocation.

Fifth, when it does this, it imparts authority to some to act on behalf of all — it does not convey any kind of supplementary priestly character as though baptized Christians lacked some priestly qualification.

Sixth, such authority (or perhaps authorization) is imparted by the body as such, for in it the fullness of priesthood resides, not by any putative ministerial order, such as bishops, within the Church — though it is fitting if fellow ministers or bishops themselves act on behalf of the Church to give sacramental expression and ratification to this authorization.

Seventh, the only proper criterion for assessing the validity of a given church's ordained ministry (that is to say, the only criterion by which we may decide whether we recognize it as a true ministry of the Church) is whether it is the reflection, expression and public manifestation of the *koinonia* — based on baptismal incorporation into Christ — of any given ecclesial body. In other words, where Churches officially recognize each other's baptisms, as in fact they do, and find a growing awareness of common ground between each other's experience of *koinonia*, there is nothing to stop — and everything to encourage — the extension of that convergence in *koinonia* to mutual recognition of ministries and sacraments, i.e. to intercommunion. This will not be enough to provide a basis for plenary, structured union between episcopal and non-episcopal Churches — other considerations beside validity come into the picture at this stage — but such unqualified mutual acceptance as Christians and as Churches is the only conceivable basis on which to mount negotiations leading to fuller unity.

The Roman Catholic Church recognizes the baptisms of Anglicans and protestants, but not their ministries. Anglicans recognize the baptisms of protestants but not their ministries. Obviously they have not yet come to appreciate the theological dynamic and momentum of the theology of baptism which leads on inexorably to ministries in communion.

7

Communion
in the Gospel?

St Paul thanked God for the Philippian Christians' '*koinonia* in the gospel' — the partnership, fellowship and support that he had received in his apostolic mission of proclaiming the gospel of the cross of Christ. They were joint partakers (*sunkoinonous*) with Paul in the grace he had received for the defence and vindication of the gospel (Philippians 1.5, 7; cf. Romans 15.26; 2 Corinthians 9.13). That gospel was an objective reality that Paul and his partners were called to share in proclaiming and promoting. The Philippians' involvement had gone beyond moral support to generous practical assistance. At the inception of his mission ('the beginning of the gospel') in mainland Greece, they had entered into partnership (*ekoinonesen*) with Paul 'in giving and receiving' — presumably, he contributing the preaching of the gospel and they contributing material provision (4.15; cf. Martin, *NCBC*, pp. 64ff., 165f.). The gospel had created communion; the gospel demanded communion; without communion the gospel would be thwarted in its mission. Communion in the gospel emerges as a fundamental dimension of the New Testament's picture of *koinonia*.

Communion in the gospel requires agreement on the doctrine of justification

In the Western Christian tradition, the Church's theological understanding of the gospel has been largely expressed in terms of justification. It is justification that has emerged as the doctrine that decides whether or not we do enjoy communion in the gospel. There are complex historical reasons for this that we need not go into now (among them, no doubt, the legal bent of the Latin mind), but the centrality of justification can also appeal to the place that this doctrine holds in the early epistles of Paul, especially Galatians and Romans. From New Testament times to today the gospel has been interpreted in terms of justification. The connection with communion has also been fundamental from the first. As Paul insists in Galatians 2, justification is a matter of whom you have table fellowship with (cf. Wright, p. 22).

For Luther justification was the criterion of the integrity of the

Church: 'If this article stands, the Church stands; if it falls, the Church falls' (*WA* 40 III, p. 352.3; cf. the later Lutheran formula; *articulus stantis aut cadentis ecclesiae*). It was the key principle of Christian doctrine — 'master and chief, Lord, ruler and judge of every kind of doctrine, which preserves and directs every doctrine of the Church' (*WA* 39 I, p. 205.2f.). As Luther put it in the Smalcald Articles (1537):

> Nothing in this article can be given up or compromised, even if heaven and earth and things temporal should be destroyed. . . . On this article rests all that we teach and practise against the pope, the devil and the world. Therefore we must be quite certain and have no doubts about it. Otherwise all is lost and the pope, the devil and all our adversaries will gain the victory. (*BC*, p. 292)

Luther was prepared to compromise on many areas of belief and practice provided justification was safeguarded. He would even be reconciled to the papacy (and 'kiss the Pope's feet': *WA* 1, p. 191) if the Pope would preach the gospel. Hooker put it less polemically when he described justification as 'that grand question, which hangeth yet in controversy between us and the Church of Rome' (3, p. 486).

Nothing that has occurred between the sixteenth and twentieth centuries has served to make the question less pressing. While Lutheran–Reformed and Anglican–Lutheran conversations were able to take agreement on justification for granted (Meyer), it might have been thought that, when at last doctrinal conversations began between the Roman Catholic and Anglican communions, the nature of the gospel and of justification in particular would have been near the top of the agenda. But surprisingly, ARCIC I did not follow this approach. It did not set out to ask such questions as: What is the gospel? How are we saved? What is fundamental in Christianity? What truths need to be believed for salvation? What constitutes a Christian community? What more, if anything, is necessary for valid orders and sacraments? If the 'essence of Christianity' approach had been pursued, the issues at stake might seem clearer to us now. If ARCIC I had adopted such a method, it could hardly have avoided tackling justification at an early stage. But instead, the commission chose to engage with problems of doctrinal agreement across a broad front, with some resulting loss of coherence. The introduction to the *Final Report* (1981) observed that 'controversy between our communions has centred on the eucharist, on the meaning and function of ordained ministry, and on the nature and exercise of authority in the Church' (p. 5). The omission of justification from this catalogue was glaring and inexplicable. With the publication of *Salvation and the Church* (1987) the omission has been rectified.

In Chapter 4, I argued that extensive agreement in doctrine was not required for intercommunion. But that is not to say that *no* doctrinal agreement is required. If we see baptism as the foundational sacrament that unites us to Christ and to each other, we have to recognize that the act of baptism itself makes a theological statement. The message of baptism is made explicit in the baptismal liturgy and particularly in the baptismal profession of faith. We turn to Christ; we repent of our sins; we renounce evil. We confess that we believe and trust in Father, Son and Holy Spirit: Creator, Redeemer and source of grace. The pouring of water symbolizes new birth to eternal life, cleansing of sins and the refreshment of divine grace. Through submersion in the element of water we are incorporated into the death and the resurrection of Christ — his crucified and risen body. Baptism is called a sacrament of the gospel, not only because it is a dominical sacrament with a mandate in the gospels, or even because it constitutes Christian initiation, but because it speaks eloquently of the truth of the gospel, the good news of God's saving grace through Christ.

Few would deny that justification is concerned with the heart of the gospel. If our communion is to be in the gospel, there must be agreement on what the gospel is — and that means agreement on justification. The Lutheran–Roman Catholic commission in the United States announced its agreement on justification in 1983 as a 'fundamental consensus on the gospel', acknowledging that such agreement was necessary 'to give credibility' to their previous agreed statements on baptism, the eucharist and ministry, and primacy (164). ARCIC II, noting that at the time of the Reformation justification was 'a particular cause of contention', speaks of the 'widespread view that the subject of justification is so central to the Christian faith that, unless there is assurance of agreement on this issue, there can be no full doctrinal agreement between our two Churches' (*SC*, p. 6). The 1988 Lambeth Conference warmly welcomed *Salvation and the Church* as 'a timely and significant contribution' to our understanding of 'the heart of the Christian faith' (L88, p. 211). So while the significance of the doctrine seems to be lost on most clergy and laity, and synodical activists seem to regard debates on justification pragmatically as an attempt to shift barriers from the past that have now lost their meaning, theologians need to insist that, in spite of its sometimes rebarbative terminology, the doctrine of justification does go to the heart of the Christian gospel.

The extent of agreement on the doctrine of justification reached between Lutherans and Roman Catholics in the USA in 1983 and between Anglicans and Roman Catholics worldwide in 1987 is impressive. It remains for the Lutheran, Anglican and Roman

Catholic authorities to decide whether these formulae of agreement are consistent with the doctrinal commitments of their traditions. It is salutary to be reminded from time to time that ecumenical dialogues are not negotiations between delegates but conversations between representatives. This point has been highlighted by an exchange of views between the late Bishop John Moorman, a member of ARCIC I, and Archbishop Henry McAdoo, Anglican co-chairman of ARCIC I. Moorman suggested (in a letter to the *Church Times* 28 November 1986) that compromise and the exchange of concessions necessarily play a part in reaching an ecumenical agreement. In response, McAdoo (*Church Times* 9 January 1987) denied that compromise and concession were involved and insisted that the Anglican and Roman Catholic members of the commission set out to explore together the teachings of the gospels (not the epistles?) and the common ancient traditions. They happily experienced a convergence of views and discovered an ecumenical consensus.

I must say that this does seem a rather idealized account of ecumenical dialogue. There is bound to be compromise in reaching an agreement between any two parties whose interests do not exactly coincide (if they did coincide, they would not be two parties but one). There is nothing unethical or otherwise objectionable in compromise. Any future form of Church unity will inevitably involve concessions on both (or all) sides. But this was not part of ARCIC's remit, as McAdoo rightly implies. Concessions and compromises belong to negotiations; partners in theological conversations are not negotiators and are not authorized to trade concessions. That role, if and when it is required, will belong to the governing bodies of the Churches concerned, or their delegates appointed for precisely that purpose.

However, when it appears that concessions *have* been made and compromises *have* been struck, one is bound to conclude that the participants have become confused about their role. There are points in the *Final Report* where what the commission would like us to see as convergence in the truth looks, even to the charitable reader, suspiciously like a negotiated compromise. The question of papal primacy is the most striking example (though not the only one: the notion of indefectibility amounting to inerrancy, sponsored by the commission, has the most tenuous basis in the Anglican tradition and has every appearance of being an attempt by the Anglican representatives to meet Roman Catholic commitments half-way).

Both the Reformers and later Anglican divines saw no insuperable objection to accepting a primacy of honour (though not, needless to say, a universal jurisdiction) for the bishop of Rome, provided that this primacy was understood as being not of divine right, but a purely *human* arrangement which the Church was entitled to make for the sake of peace and unity. ARCIC I renounces the rhetoric of divine right, acknowledging that there is no sound basis in the New Testament for a perpetual Petrine office in the Church. But the commission nevertheless proposes that papal primacy should be accepted for any united Church of the future on the grounds that it is a part of the divine intention and purpose as revealed through the providential ordering of Church history (*FR*, pp. 83ff.). Let us leave aside all the difficulties entailed in claiming that we know what the will of God is, except as it is revealed in scripture, and set aside also the weaknesses inherent in any appeal to the workings of providence in history (are the Eastern Churches equally providential? the Reformation? the Old Catholics? Methodism?). My objection is that to appeal to the will of God manifested through his providential ordering of history is to introduce divine right by the back door. If the papacy is the will of God, and we can know that it is, whether through scripture or providence, woe betide all who resist his will.

Christian beliefs have traditionally been divided into 'things necessary to salvation' (as the Thirty-nine Articles characteristically put it) and things indifferent (*adiaphora*), fundamentals and non-fundamentals (see Avis, *Anglicanism*; Sykes in Sykes and Booty (eds)). The Second Vatican Council spoke of a 'hierarchy of truths' (V2, p. 354). The essence of Christianity project has operated with a tacit distinction between what is essential to Christianity and what is non-essential.

So if the papal office (whether seen in terms of universal immediate jurisdiction or merely in terms of a primacy of honour, a presidency by consent) is the will of God for his Church it can hardly be treated as non-fundamental, non-essential, an *adiaphoron*. It inevitably moves right up the hierarchy of truths for all Christians. It begins to impinge on the area of truths necessary for salvation. It becomes non-negotiable. Thus, by accepting the concept of a papacy by divine right, by the back door of the providential ordering of history, the Anglican representatives on ARCIC I gave away at a stroke what the Churches of the Reformation, including the Anglican Church, had consistently and discriminatingly upheld for 400 years.

Hardly a voice was heard to protest at this unwitting betrayal of Anglican principle. But a fudging of the issues on justification would not escape censure. Evangelicals, who are weak on ecclesiology, are strong on soteriology and would be vigilant. On the question of justification there can be no compromise. In my view ARCIC II has not indulged in it — but the Sacred Congregation for the Doctrine of the Faith is not so sure!

In its 'Observations' (1988), which had the approval of Pope John Paul II, the SCDF made a 'substantially positive' evaluation of

Salvation and the Church but criticized it for 'ambiguous formulations', 'vagueness' and 'weakness'. It found its figurative or 'symbolic' language difficult to interpret univocally. It was capable of being interpreted 'in a way that conforms with Catholic faith' — but not unambiguously so. This meant that the SCDF could not ratify the conclusion of the report that the two communions were agreed on the essential aspects of this doctrine. Altogether this authoritative comment insisted on greater precision and clarification.

The less authoritative 'Commentary' on the observations insisted that the commission should have employed 'more rigorous doctrinal formulations, though not necessarily scholastic ones' and suggested that the commission would have performed a service if it had set out in a separate protocol the areas of remaining differences. The SCDF obviously thought that its criticisms of ARCIC I had not been heeded, for once again it requested more explicit attention to the documentary sources of the respective traditions — 'particularly to the Fathers, and to the Magisterium of the Catholic Church, as well as to the official acts of the Anglican Communion', such as the Thirty-nine Articles.

ARCIC I had set out to avoid this approach: ARCIC II has compromised with it and established a sort of half-way house. The preface to the *Final Report* of ARCIC I reiterated the principles that had guided its procedure. 'From the beginning', it stated, 'we were determined, in accordance with our mandate and in the spirit of Philippians 3.13, "forgetting what lies behind and straining forward to what lies ahead", to discover each other's faith as it is today and to appeal to history only for enlightenment, not as a way of perpetuating past controversy' (*FR*, pp. 1f.). In line with this policy, specific reference in the text of the agreements to the doctrinal formularies of the two communions was minimal. This has given rise to frustration on both sides. On the Roman Catholic side Cardinal Ratzinger and the SCDF have requested greater reference to the Anglican confessional documents. On the Anglican side, I for one have argued that the historical sources embody the corporate memories of their Churches and I have suggested that if agreed statements were to set out frankly and fully the areas of remaining disagreement, as well as the areas where common ground had been discovered, they would perform a more valuable service to ecumenism in the long run (Avis, *Ecum. Theol.*, esp. pp. x, 44).

On this score, ARCIC II is more satisfactory than its predecessor: it does indeed provide more extensive reference to both Roman Catholic and Anglican formularies. This serves to guard against ambiguity on the part of the agreed statement and misunderstanding on the part of its readers. A mandate for this approach is found in the essay 'The reconciliation of memories' by Mark Santer the Anglican co-chairman (in Santer (ed.)) where he speaks impressively of Christians fearlessly facing the past together and re-educating their memories of each other. Contrary to the assumption of ARCIC I, bringing the past to light need not be a way of perpetuating old controversies. As G. M. Trevelyan wrote, 'The study of past controversies of which the final outcome is known destroys the spirit of prejudice' (p. 153).

The early agreements of ARCIC I (on the eucharist and the ministry) were far too short. *Salvation and the Church* is longer but not long enough. Allowing for repetition, which in this sensitive area is not perhaps superfluous, and flights of eloquence — again appropriate when the substance·of the gospel is being proclaimed — the statement is still not full enough for informed study and response. I would have liked an even more concise agreed statement without some of the rhetoric but accompanied by more extensive references to Trent and the Anglican formularies. For example, we are told that 'Anglican theologians reacted to the decree of the Council of Trent on justification in a variety of ways, some sympathetic, others critical at least on particular points' (p. 10). Though this is followed by a note of the versions of the decree now available and of the principal Anglican documents and authors before 1661, the text here is far too vague. What does it mean that they were 'sympathetic'? And there was not a single Anglican divine who was not critical of Trent 'at least on particular points'. This is one weak spot and it is not typical: but can I make a plea for fuller and more precise documentation? Here, somewhat to my surprise, I find myself consistently in agreement with the SCDF.

Ecumenical theology has placed historical differences over justification in a new perspective

During the past thirty years, a remarkable *rapprochement* has taken place between separated Christian traditions over the doctrine of justification. It began with Hans Küng's pioneering work *Justification* (1957; ET 1964; new edition 1981) which was a dialogue with the doctrine of Karl Barth — agreement between Roman Catholic and Reformed. Between 1976 and 1982 Lutherans and Roman Catholics in the USA thrashed out their differences, resulting in the substantial report *Justification by Faith* (1983) — agreement between the heirs of Luther and the heirs of Cardinal Bellarmine! In 1986 the Anglican evangelical scholar Alister McGrath published his indispensable *Iustitia Dei* which pointed towards similar encouraging conclusions. In the following year (1987) ARCIC II produced its first piece of work, the report *Salvation and the Church*. This is the clearest brief statement of the issues and of how historical conflicts may be resolved. Let us now turn to this document.

The keynote of *Salvation and the Church* is clear from the start: the heart of the gospel proclaimed by the Church is 'salvation through the grace of God in Christ'; Roman Catholics and Anglicans are unanimous that salvation is due 'solely to the mercy and grace of God' responded to in faith (1, 3). The theme of pure unmerited grace is dominant from first to last. The difficulties — and the substances of the commission's task — begin with the work of comparing the decree of the Council of Trent with the Anglican formularies (i.e. Articles 11–14 of the Thirty-nine and Cranmer's homily 'Of Salvation', to which Article 11 refers, together with the 'classical' interpreters of the Anglican doctrine of justification: Hooker, Field, Andrewes, Davenant, Hall, Beveridge, etc.). Here the 16 sections and 33 anathemas of Trent contrast with the conciseness and simplicity of the Anglican Articles which testify to the characteristic Anglican reticence in the matter of dogma. This is one of those differences of theological horizon that constitute the submerged part of the iceberg of ecumenical theology, lurking in the waters of ecumenical endeavour, that may one day make its presence all too apparent with disastrous consequences (cf. Avis. *Ecum. Theol.,* pp. xiif.).

The statement suggests that the conflict between Reformation and Anglican views of justification on the one hand, and the doctrine of Trent on the other is largely attributable to differences of terminology, mutual misunderstanding and a tendency to caricature the opposition. Drawing on the humanist study of the Greek New Testament, Protestants recovered the authentically Pauline forensic meaning of justification as to declare righteous. Roman Catholics on the other hand, following the Latin Vulgate and Augustine, took justification (*iustificare*) as meaning to make righteous (*iustum facere*).

Accordingly, the Reformers and later Anglican divines define justification as the act of reconciliation flowing from the grace of God through the imputation of Christ's righteousness or merits to the sinner and received by faith irrespective of any progress in holiness. Roman Catholic doctrine regards justification as equivalent to the whole process of salvation, not just its inception, as flowing from the grace of God and as taking effect through the infusion of the righteousness of God into the soul, not as of human merit but solely on account of the merits of Christ. The vital conceptual distinction which the Reformers made between justification and sanctification was intended to safeguard the unmerited givenness of divine grace, but it was open to being misunderstood as devaluing the need for holiness 'without which no man shall see the Lord' and the fruits of a regenerate life. The Reformers' stress on the external, 'alien', 'not my own', imputed character of justifying righteousness was intended to cut through the merit-mongering of later medieval popular religion, but it was taken by the fathers of the Council of Trent to imply that no actual change was involved.

If the Reformers emphasized the truth 'He died that we might be forgiven', Trent was concerned to stress the truth 'He died to make us good'. The Reformers' watchword *sola fide* was intended to suggest 'nothing in my hand I bring, simply to thy cross I cling'. Faith was merely receptive, the subjective appropriation of the benefits of Christ. In Trent's anathema on justification by faith alone, faith was interpreted as a vain human boasting confidence that we are justified. Roman Catholics did not deny imputation, but it was radically subordinate to impartation. Protestants did not dispute infusion — this was inseparable from their doctrine of union with Christ — but it was not on the basis of any infused righteousness that we were justified in the sight of God. For Catholics justification was eschatological: it looked forward to our ultimate redemption, our hoped for acquittal at the Last Judgement, when good works and actual righteousness would not be irrelevant. For Protestants justification was immanent; it was realized eschatology; even now through our union with Christ we are seated with him in heavenly places. If Protestants responded to distortions of Catholic doctrine in popular piety, distortions not sufficiently discouraged by the Church, Catholics reacted to distortions of Protestant teaching, distortions that polemic and popularization had tended to invite. But the fact remains that Reformation theology had recovered the authentic Pauline meaning of justification as a forensic or juridical term; the appropriation of this in modern Roman Catholic scholarship is conducive to a new mutual understanding.

The statement concludes that in the central area of the doctrine of salvation there need be no dispute. Any differences of interpretation or emphasis that may remain are not sufficient in themselves to justify the continued separation of the communions. 'Our two communions are agreed on the essential aspects of the doctrine of salvation' (32).

The consensus that has now emerged, between Roman Catholics on the one hand and Lutherans and Anglicans on the other, includes the following points.

a Salvation is wholly of grace — it is the gift of God on account of Christ and cannot be earned.

b Salvation is appropriated by faith which involves both belief in the gospel and a personal response of commitment and obedience.

c The source of our salvation is the righteousness of God which in the Bible is not the righteousness that judges and condemns, but the righteousness that God graciously bestows upon us.

d The Pauline meaning of justification is forensic and means to declare or reckon righteous. This insight was recovered from the Greek New Testament by the Reformers. For the tradition of Latin Christianity following Augustine, on the other hand, justification was used in a performative sense, meaning to make righteous.

e Justification and sanctification need to be clearly distinguished. For Protestants, justification was the decisive act of God's reconciliation of us to his favour and was followed by a period of growth in grace and holiness — the process of sanctification. For Roman Catholics, on the other hand, sanctification was included in justification which embraced the whole process of salvation. The new consensus recognizes that sanctification is inseparable from justification (in the Protestant sense) because God's word is creative, and in declaring righteous it must make us righteous.

f The righteousness of God is both imputed and imparted. But if it is asked, on the basis of which righteousness are we justified — imputed or imparted?, we first have to ask whether 'justified' here is being used in the Protestant or in the Roman Catholic sense. If justification refers to the divine act of reconciliation that initiates our Christian life, then we must say that we are justified solely through the imputed righteousness of Christ. But if justification refers to the lifelong process of salvation, then we have to say that we are 'justified' on the ground of the real imparted righteousness of Christ also, 'for without holiness no one shall see the Lord' (Hebrews 12.14).

g Our sanctification is progressive and always imperfect, necessitating daily repentance and renewal.

h The Christian's heavenly reward is a gift of divine grace. The traditional Catholic language of merit is not meant to imply that we can ever place God in our debt.

This summary is particularly indebted to *Salvation and the Church* where the issues are more sharply focused than in *Justification by Faith* — though the latter is more satisfying in the amount of theological and historical material it adduces for its conclusions. Altogether, this is an impressive and encouraging consensus. However, we cannot assume without further enquiry that it is consistent with the Roman Catholic and Anglican traditions. To the task of comparison and evaluation we now turn.

Not all substantial differences between the Tridentine and the Protestant doctrines of justification can be attributed to misunderstandings and differences of terminology

The conclusions of ARCIC II on justification had been anticipated by Hans Küng 30 years before. 'Protestants speak of a declaration of justice and Catholics of a making just. But Protestants speak of a declaring just which includes a making just; and Catholics of a making just which supposes a declaring just. Is it not time to stop arguing about imaginary differences?' (*Justification*, p. 221). Küng also warned about the danger of misunderstanding each other's terminology, pointing out that what Protestants call justification, many Roman Catholics call redemption (p. 227). This point was echoed in the Lutheran–Roman Catholic document *Justification by Faith* (1983) which stated:

> Many of the difficulties have arisen from the contrasting concerns and patterns of thought in the two traditions. In the polemical atmosphere of the past these differences gave rise to fears and were interpreted as conflicts, but the development of ecumenical dialogue, historical research and new modes of theological thinking enable us to consider the possibility that these patterns may in part be complementary and, even if at times in unavoidable tension, not necessarily divisive. (94)

At the end of his two-volume historical survey of the doctrine of justification, Alister McGrath came to a similar conclusion:

> Increasingly precise historical investigation of the origins of the Reformation and the nature of the sixteenth-century debates on justification has led to the recognition that many of the disputed questions on justification involved conceptual differences, or differences in emphasis, rather than substantial disagreement on the basic question of salvation. (2, p. 189)

In this section I want to look at some criticisms of the Tridentine decree on justification and to ask whether they really can be resolved by recognizing different viewpoints and vocabulary.

Richard Hooker, for example, acknowledged much common ground with the Roman doctrine. 'They teach as we do' is Hooker's oft-repeated refrain when he reviews the Tridentine teaching, and he concludes, 'Thus far we join hands with the Church of Rome' ('Sermon on Justification, etc', 4: 3, p. 486). Hooker and the English divines welcomed Trent's insistence that justification cannot be merited: 'nothing that precedes justification, neither faith nor works, merits (*promeretur*) the grace of justification' (DS 1532: *CF* 1935); that the human response of faith is required: ' "faith is the beginning of man's salvation", the foundation and root of all justification' (DS

1532: *CF* 1935); that prevenient grace enables the believer to make this response of faith: 'without God's grace, he cannot by his own free will take one step towards justice in God's sight' (DS 1525: *CF* 1929); that the merits of Christ are the only source of our justification: 'no one can be just unless the merits of the passion of our Lord Jesus Christ are imparted (*communicantur*) to him' (DS 1930: *CF* 1933).

'Where then do we disagree?' asks Hooker. His reply gives the lie to any glib assumption that the 'grand question which hangeth yet in controversy between us and the Church of Rome' can be explained as a series of misunderstandings. 'We disagree', Hooker replies, 'about the nature of the very essence of the medicine whereby Christ cureth our disease; about the manner of applying it; about the number and power of means, which God requireth in us for the effectual applying thereof to our soul's comfort' ('Sermon on Justification, etc', 5: 3, p. 486). What Hooker fundamentally objects to is the Roman Catholic doctrine that justification is by inherent, rather than imputed, grace.

Hooker is well aware that Roman Catholics use 'justification' to refer to the whole process of the Christian's growth in grace and holiness — there is no misunderstanding here — but he also knows that that does not exclude its use to refer to the inception of the Christian life. He reminds his readers that Roman theologians speak of a first and second justification. Though this expression does not appear in the Tridentine decree, the substance of it certainly does. After describing the role of prevenient grace and human response in preparing the individual for conversion, repentance and baptism, the decree goes on: 'This disposition or preparation is followed by justification itself, which is not [only] the remission of sins but [also] the sanctification and renewal of the interior man through the voluntary reception of grace and of the gifts, whereby from unjust man becomes just' (DS 1528, *non est sola peccatorum remissio, sed et sanctificatio et renovatio*, etc.: *CF* 1932 — a misleading translation). Hooker comments: 'Whether they speak of the first or second justification, they make the essence of it a divine quality inherent, they make it righteousness which is in us'. Hooker finds this hard to reconcile with Philippians 3.9: 'not having my own righteousness' ('Sermon on Justification, etc', 6: 3, p. 490).

Another way of putting it was to employ the Aristotelian and scholastic vocabulary of causation and this Trent does, though on the whole it tends to eschew scholastic categories. The *final*, teleological cause is the glory of God and of Christ and life everlasting. The *efficient*, operative cause is the mercy of God working through the Holy Spirit. The *meritorious* cause, on account of which our justification becomes possible, is Jesus Christ who merited salvation for us through his passion and made satisfaction to the Father on our behalf. The *instrumental* cause, that enables us to receive the benefit of

Christ's merits, is baptism, the sacrament of faith: 'without which [faith] no one has ever been justified'. With all this Hooker and the Anglican divines could gladly concur. It is the next clause that is the bone of contention. The single *formal* cause (*unica formalis causa*) is the justice or righteousness of God (*iustitia Dei*), 'not that by which he himself is just, but that by which he makes us just' (Augustine). Even this Protestants could accept: was not Augustine's insight into the righteousness of God the key to Luther's breakthrough? But Trent goes on to define this justice as 'the justice which we have as a gift from him and by which we are spiritually renewed (*renovamur spiritu mentis nostrae*)' and concludes: 'Thus, not only are we considered just (*non modo reputamur*) but we are truly called just and we are just (*sed vere iusti nominamur et sumus*), each one receiving within himself his own justice' (DS 1529: *CF* 1932).

On this crucial statement there are several critical observations that need to be made.

First, the insistence on a single formal cause (*unica formalis causa*) was a deliberate attempt to close pre-Tridentine debate which would have allowed for a double (*duplex*) justice, a two-fold justification — both imputed and imparted. This formula was not what Luther had in mind in his notably unclear sermon on 'Two kinds of righteousness' in 1518–19 (*LW*, 31, pp. 297–306) but it had been favoured at the Colloquy of Regensburg (or Ratisbon) in 1541 and had been advocated by Seripando during the proceedings at Trent leading up to the decree. The double justice concept has recently been revived by ecumenical theologians of the weight of Henry Chadwick ('Justification by faith'), Edward Yarnold ('Duplex iustitia' in Evans (ed.)), and Bruno Brinkman (pp. 245f.). The Lutheran–Roman Catholic agreement in the USA flirted with it when it spoke of imputed and imparted righteousness as 'complementary' (94, 158). But it seems to me that Trent acted entirely logically in excluding this concept. Trent did not want to concede that justification could be purely imputative at any stage, or that imputation could be divorced, even conceptually, from the impartation of actual righteousness. It is salutary to recall that both Luther and papal assessors rejected the Regensburg formula as ambiguous. Since Trent excluded it and ARCIC II has not explicitly employed it, it would seem rather quixotic to start toying with it now.

Second, though Trent does not absolutely rule out the forensic sense of justification, it does rule it out except in inseparable conjunction with real inherent righteousness. Canon 11 condemns those who claim that individuals 'are justified either by the imputation of Christ's justice alone, or by the remission of sins alone, excluding grace and charity which is poured into their hearts by the Holy Spirit and inheres in them, or also that the grace which justifies us is only the favour of God' (DS 1561: *CF* 1961). Though the Reformers are not named, there is an implied assumption that Protestants taught that the Christian life could begin and continue without any inner transformation of the sinner — and this is a grotesque caricature of the truth (cf. McGrath, *Iustitia Dei*, 2, p. 85).

Third, the Reformers found the Tridentine doctrine logically inconsistent. As McGrath has put it: if justification was not to be a legal fiction, it would have to be based on a perfect righteousness. But if this perfect righteousness was inherent, how could Trent speak of a growth in righteousness (McGrath, *ARCIC II*, p. 22)? This is precisely why the Reformers insisted that inherent righteousness was imperfect and could not be the ground of justification.

Fourth, the Reformers believed that Trent entailed a woefully inadequate doctrine of sin remaining in the believer. Whereas for Luther, for example, human sinfulness was an ineradicable state of self-centredness (*curvatus in se*) infecting one's whole being, which ensured that one would always fall short of the glory of God, for Trent remaining concupiscence was not sin unless freely assented to. For Trent, you were either in a state of grace which banished sin, or in a state of sin which banished grace. Trent could not accommodate Luther's insight: *simul iustus et peccator* — the Christian as a justified sinner. The Reformers believed that Tridentine teaching on this point was pastorally disastrous (cf. C. F. Allison, 'Pastoral and political implications'; Brinkman, pp. 262f.).

Finally, it followed from this that Tridentine doctrine was anthropologically inadequate. Bruno Brinkman has evaluated the Lutheran and Tridentine doctrines of justification for their anthropological adequacy (ch. 7). His thesis is that they embody opposing anthropologies which undermine today's ecumenical consensus based on pursuit of the common ground. Trent reinforced an anachronistic medieval anthropology. Tridentine man is a theoretical construct whose nature — dominantly intellectual — is given *a priori*, and whose sins are detached acts. Luther, on the other hand, initiated an anthropological revolution. Martinian man is concrete and dynamic. His existence is his becoming. He wrestles with God in temptations and his sin is a state of being. Tridentine man is a bad theologian and ecumenist, for neither are purely intellectual matters. But Martinian man is a model theologian, even for Roman Catholics. He agonizes to grasp the truth of God incarnate in worldly existence. He seeks his freedom from God — a freedom that is located at his point of need. The question he asks is not 'What is man?', but 'Where is man?' — where is he before God, *coram Deo*?

The Reformers' objections to the Tridentine decree were thus fundamentally directed to the doctrine of a single formal cause of justification, the infusion of actual and inherent righteousness which formed the basis of divine acceptance and could be lost by mortal sin, depleted by venial sins, and supplemented by meritorious works. It was, in their judgement, ultimately responsible for the whole mercenary carnival of medieval merit-mongering and its corresponding confusion, fear, and exploitation of the laity. Hooker is implacable:

This is the mystery of the man of sin. This maze the Church of Rome doth cause her followers to tread, when they ask her the way of justification. . . . The Church of Rome, in teaching justification by inherent grace, doth pervert the truth of Christ. . . . The doctrine professed in the church of Rome doth bereave men of comfort, both in their lives, and at their deaths. ('Sermon on Justification etc.', 5, 6, 9: 3, pp. 489, 491, 495)

In conclusion, as Alister McGrath has repeatedly pointed out, as well as differences of approach and terminology that are capable of being reconciled, there are also real disagreements of substance — and we do ecumenism no service by brushing them under the carpet. The crucial disagreement was over the formal cause of justification. Though neither Trent nor Bellarmine denied the role of imputation in justification, it was not pivotal in their doctrine: they would not make it the formal cause. That remained the infusion of the perfect righteousness of God through the merits of Christ. The Reformers objected fundamentally to this interpretation. They held it to be unbiblical, unevangelical and unpastoral — contrary to Scripture, the Christian gospel and pastoral requirements. They maintained that it led to errors concerning merit, penance, indulgences, works of supererogation, and sin remaining in the believer. Richard Field argued with massive learning that the question of the formal cause of justification had been left open in Catholic theology before Trent. By foreclosing the matter and rejecting the true insights of the Reformers, Trent had become an apostate faction within the Catholic Church (Appendix to III.11: 2, pp. 318ff.; 4, pp. 485ff.). But this did not lead the Reformers to deny Rome to be a Christian Church in which the gospel was known and the way of salvation was to be found. Hooker insisted against the puritans that Rome held the foundation of the faith, erring in 'a consequent', an inference, a deduction from the essential gospel. In so far as the Roman Catholic Church is still committed, as it surely is, to the decree of the Council of Trent, that must remain the Anglican position. In my estimate, ARCIC II's *Salvation and the Church* is not reconcilable with a strict interpretation of Trent — it was generous of the SCDF to suggest that it might be capable of being so interpreted. But even if not, it would be a defensible Anglican position to hold that sufficient progress has been made in confirming and strengthening that fundamental agreement on the foundation of faith, of which Hooker spoke, for disagreements on justification and related issues no longer to be a barrier to intercommunion. It is devoutly to be hoped that the Vatican will take the same view!

The Anglican theological tradition exhibits a consensus on the doctrine of justification against which ecumenical agreement can be measured

The doctrine of justification — for Luther the *articulus stantis vel cadentis ecclesiae* and for Hooker the 'grand question' in dispute between Canterbury and Rome — was for the first Doctrine Commission of the Church of England, in its report *Doctrine in the Church of England* (1938), not worth mentioning. Here, however, the Archbishops' Commission was not representative of the Anglican tradition, which has not been remiss in attending to the matter of justification. Though there are pronounced oscillations of emphasis on this question, with Bishop Bull and Newman on one side and Hooker and Maurice on the other, a consensus can be discerned which, though in certain respects catholic in form, is definitely evangelical in spirit. After Newman's challenge to the tradition, equilibrium was regained in the catholic movement within the Church of England. The consensus of Anglican theology on the question of justification provides a touchstone against which the reconciling formulae produced by ARCIC II can be measured. Let us briefly pass in review some of the historical milestones in the Anglican engagement with justification.

The Thirty-nine Articles make only a perfunctory reference to justification — more of an assertion than a definition. Article 11 simply says:

> We are accounted righteous before God, only for the merit of our Lord and Saviour Jesus Christ by Faith, and not for our own works or deservings: Wherefore that we are justified by Faith only is a most wholesome Doctrine, and very full of comfort, as more largely is expressed in the Homily of Justification.

This article keeps a courteous distance from both Protestant orthodoxy and Trent. Neither the article, nor the homily (actually 'Of salvation') employs the concept of imputation of Christ's righteousness. In this omission the article follows the corresponding statement of the Lutheran Augsburg Confession (1530) of which it appears to be an attenuated version. The homily, reputedly by Cranmer himself, is an example of the classical Anglican gift of theological discrimination. 'Faith doth not shut out repentance, hope, love, dread and the fear of God, to be joined with faith in every man that is justified, but it shutteth them out from the office of justifying.'

Article 12 'Of good works' corrects what was believed to be the deficiency of Luther's approach, the disparagement of works, while insisting that works cannot justify:

> Albeit that Good Works, which are the fruits of Faith, and follow after Justification, cannot put away our sins, and endure the severity of God's Judgement, yet are they pleasing and acceptable to God in Christ, and do spring out necessarily of a true and lively Faith.

Thus the Articles pursue a middle way, preserving the independence of the English Church from both Luther and Rome. They state the essentials in a constructive, pastoral and non-polemical way. The Anglican Reformers themselves did not follow Luther closely. The earlier Reformers, notably Barnes and Tyndale, tended to be Erasmian, moralistic and legalistic — closer to Rome than to Luther (Clebsch, pp. 68, 311–17), the later English Reformers being more indebted to the clear and sound definitions of justification stemming from Swiss Reformed theology, following Calvin.

Richard Hooker's doctrine of justification (in his 'Learned discourse', corroborated by occasional references in the *Laws of Ecclesiastical Polity*), while it employs scholastic terminology, remains pure evangelical theology. Hooker's magisterial clarity cuts through so much confusion and ambiguity in the sixteenth-century discussion of justification.

> There is a glorifying righteousness of men in the world to come: and there is a justifying and a sanctifying righteousness here. The righteousness, wherewith we shall be clothed in the world to come, is both perfect and inherent. That whereby we are justified is perfect but not inherent. That whereby we are sanctified, inherent but not perfect. ('Justification': 3, p. 485)

In an earlier sermon, the second of the two on Jude, Hooker speaks in an even more distinctly Protestant vein:

> We are justified by faith. . . . Being justified, all our iniquities are covered; God beholdeth us in the righteousness which is imputed, and not in the sins which we have committed. . . . It is true we are full of sin, both original and actual. . . . But imputation of righteousness hath covered the sins of every soul which believeth. . . . Justification washeth away sin; sin removed, we are clothed with the righteousness which is of God; the righteousness of God maketh us most holy. (Sermon VI, 23–28: 3, pp. 693f.)

And there is something that we find in the great Protestant divines of the sheer miracle of it all: 'To make a wicked and sinful man most holy through his believing, is more than to create a world of nothing' (ibid.).

Hooker speaks of justifying faith in terms that echo the Homily of Salvation:

> To the imputation of Christ's death for remission of sins, we teach faith alone necessary: wherein it is not our meaning to separate thereby faith from any other quality or duty, which God requireth to be matched herewith, but from faith to seclude in justification the fellowship of worth through precedent works. . . . Nor doth any faith justify, but that wherewith there is joined both hope and love. (*EP*, V. App. 1: 2, p. 553)

Like the Reformers, Hooker holds the distinction between justification and sanctification to be fundamental. In using the un-Protestant concept of first and second justification (though Luther had spoken of 'Two kinds of righteousness' as a way of distinguishing between justification and sanctification: *LW*, 31, pp. 297–306), Hooker believes that he is following the Epistle of James:

> To be justified so far as remission of sins, it sufficeth if we believe what another hath wrought in us: but whosoever will see God face to face, let him show his faith by his works, demonstrate his first justification by a second. . . *Abraham was justified* (that is to say, his life was sanctified) by works. (*EP*, V. App. 1: 2, p. 553)

Here Hooker appears as the forerunner of the late seventeenth-century 'holy living' school of Anglican divines, but his evangelical cutting edge is as sharp as ever: 'We are therefore justified by faith without works, by grace without merit' (ibid.).

Hooker guards against a merely extrinsic understanding of justification when he insists that regeneration and the imputation of Christ's righteousness must be concurrent. For we cannot be justified by faith until we have faith, and we cannot exercise faith until we have the Spirit of adoption crying out to God in our hearts. Justification therefore presupposes the work of grace. Hooker calls this 'habitual righteousness' and distinguishes it not only from justifying, imputed, 'external' righteousness, but also from the 'actual' holiness which adorns the Christian life ('Justification', 21: 3, pp. 507f.; cf. Gibbs).

Hooker does not employ the notion of double justice, nor does he speak of a double justification. As we have seen, in an early sermon he speaks of first and second justification as equivalent to justification and sanctification. But in the great discourse on justification, Hooker distances himself from this terminology ('in their divinity': 'Justification', 5: 3, p. 488). On the one occasion when Hooker does deploy something like a concept of complementarity, it is not a twofold justification that he has in mind, but a twofold participation in Christ akin to Calvin's doctrine of imputed and imparted righteousness as the two contiguous dimensions of the believer's union with Christ. It is precisely in the context of the communion of saints, the *koinonia* of God, Christ and his people, that Hooker gives us, almost in passing, one of his clearest utterances on justification:

> Thus we participate Christ partly by imputation, as when those things which he did and suffered for us are imputed into us for righteousness; partly by habitual and real infusion, as when grace is inwardly bestowed while we are on earth, and afterwards more fully both our souls and bodies made like unto his in glory. (*EP*, V.lvi.11: 2, p. 254)

The consensus of Anglican divines before the Restoration follows Hooker in stressing the distinction between justification and sanctification. They insist, against Trent, that the 'formal cause' of justification is the imputed, not the infused righteousness of God through Christ. Richard Field, broadly Hooker's contemporary, writes:

> Concerning justification, there is a very main difference between the papists and us: for though we deny not but that there is a donation and giving of the Spirit to all them that are justified; changing and altering them in such sort as that they begin to do the works of righteousness; yet we teach that justification consisteth in such sort in the remission of sins, and the imputation of Christ's righteousness, that the faithful soul must trust to no other righteousness but that which is imputed; the other being imperfect and not enduring the trial of God's severe judgement. (4, p. 390)

John Davenant, in his exhaustive treatise of 1631, insisted that justification and sanctification must neither be confounded nor separated. Justification itself consists in the remission of sins and acceptance 'unto life eternal' (1, p. 211), but the justified are not merely pronounced just — they really are made just through inherent sanctification ('habitual righteousness') issuing in good works ('actual righteousness'). However, the justice of sanctification is imperfect in this life ('imperfect and incipient righteousness renders a man just, but imperfectly and inchoately': 1, p. 160) and sin (not merely non-culpable concupiscence, as Trent would have it) remains in the believer. Davenant claimed that Luther, Calvin and the English Reformers held that there is an inherent sanctification of the justified (refuting the calumny of Bellarmine that Protestants deny inherent righteousness: 1, pp. 2f.), but this is not the cause (or formal cause) of their justification.

Archbishop John Bramhall wrote in 1656: 'I do acknowledge true inherent righteousness in this life, though imperfect, by which a Christian is rendered truly just, as gold is true gold, though it be mixed with some dross'. But justification signified a legal acquittal from guilt, freedom from condemnation, by the free grace of God, through the merits of Christ, 'by the new evangelical covenant of believing' (2, p. 87).

William Beveridge gives us one of the clearest statements of the so-called 'classical' Anglican position on justification. In his exposition of the Thirty-nine Articles, published posthumously (Beveridge, who was Bishop of St Asaph, died in 1708) he produced a typically balanced and judicious definition. 'We could not be made righteous but by God's grace implanted in us. . . . We cannot be accounted righteous but by Christ's merits imputed to us' (7, p. 286). And again: 'It is not by inhesion of grace in us, but by the imputation of righteousness to us that we are justified; as it is not by the imputation of righteousness to us, but by the inhesion of grace in us that we are sanctified' (p. 287). Continuing his explanation of Article 11, Beveridge writes:

> Every one that is justified is also sanctified, and everyone that is sanctified is also justified. But yet the acts of justification and sanctification are distinct things: for the one denotes the imputation of righteousness to us; the other denotes the implantation of righteousness in us. And, therefore, though they be both acts of God, yet the one is the act of God towards us, and the other is the act of God in us. . . . By our sanctification we are made righteous in ourselves, but not accounted righteous by God; by our justification we are accounted righteous by God, but not made righteous in ourselves. (p. 289)

The clarity of thinking and the sure-footed discrimination possessed by these Caroline divines, particularly Davenant and Beveridge, perpetuates Hooker's legacy to Anglicanism. Can it not also make a contribution to the ecumenical search today? It gives precision to the more acceptable of Luther's insights. It excels Trent for clarity and absence of ambiguity. The rhetorical language of *Salvation and the Church* is not ultimately conducive to ecumenical agreement.

The late-seventeenth- and early-eighteenth-century Anglican divines exhibit a marked difference of emphasis in their treatments of justification. Reacting to the antinomianism that flourished during the Civil War and Commonwealth, and to the dissoluteness of Restoration society, they stressed repentance and obedience as human works, stemming from the divine infusion of a principle of regeneration, preparing us for justification. As we have seen, this approach could appeal to Hooker, but its first major development was by William Forbes (1585–1634), the first Bishop of Edinburgh. Forbes emphasizes that faith is fundamentally assent to revelation. Though inspired by the Holy Spirit, faith is inevitably a human work, and to deny that is 'impertinently subtle'. But, as 'all Protestants' hold, it is living faith, working by love and informed by the intention to perform good works. Of course faith, even though a work, is not meritorious, but purely instrumental: by it we apprehend and receive justification. Forbes insists that the formula 'by faith alone' should not be contended for and is not in itself a sufficient cause for separation from Rome (1, pp. 17, 23, 43, 55, 57, 89).

Forbes prefaces his discussion of the formal cause of justification with the disclaimer: 'Let us avoid subtle and scholastic disputes (among which, perchance, is this one . . .) and audacious and peremptory definitions under pain of anathema' (a swipe at the Tridentine canons) (1, p. 97). Forbes employs a conceptuality similar to the double justice formula rejected by Trent. There is but one righteousness but it is twofold. Against Trent, 'which has falsely and even inconsistently declared, that there is but one formal cause of our justification, viz., the justice infused into us — we answer, I say, that justification is an entity, one by aggregation, and compounded of two, which by necessary conjunction and coordination are one only'. The two parts are, of course, imputation and infusion, forgiveness of sins and the gift of sanctifying grace (1, pp. 205, 407). Forbes goes on, however, to insist that works, even those proceeding from faith, can never properly merit (in Roman terms, condignly merit) the increase of righteousness, 'much less eternal glory'. Forbes will have no truck with 'merits properly so called', though he insists that merit can be used in an unobjectionable sense (1, pp. 427, 431ff., 453). Forbes uses the term 'second justification', not as the early Hooker did, as a synonym for sanctification, but almost as equivalent to penance — for the forgiveness of sins following first justification and the ensuing growth in grace. Forbes's own argument is hardly exempt from the 'subtle and scholastic' habits that he claims to shun. Though his hospitality to the double justice concept may commend him to some today, it seems to me that he confuses, rather than clarifies the issues.

Henry Hammond, a pioneer of the reconstructed Anglican Church, touched on justification in his *Practical Catechism* (c. 1644). His definition reaches back to Hooker's teaching that a principle of new life is inseparable from justification, and anticipates the 'holy living' school of the early eighteenth century. Justification is the accepting of our persons and the pardoning of our sins. Hammond has no place for merit: all is of free grace. But the faith and repentance that are essential conditions of justification are evidence of the 'new life' infused by grace. This regenerate life is 'the first part of sanctification', but not equivalent to 'the sanctified state' (pp. 78ff.).

George Bull (1634–1710), Bishop of St David's, is often cited as the most favourably disposed of Anglican writers between Forbes and Newman to the Tridentine doctrine of justification. This is an over-simplification. In his dissertation on justification, Bull insists that 'to justify' is a forensic concept, 'a judicial term', signifying 'the act of

God as a judge, acquitting the accused, according to the merciful law of Christ, pronouncing him righteous, and admitting him to the reward of righteousness, that is, eternal life' (1, p. 10). The expression 'justified by works' in the Epistle of James 'does not mean that our works are the principle or meritorious cause of our justification, for that depends on the mere and gracious mercy of God the Father, while the cause thereof is to be placed solely in the death and merits of Christ' (ibid.). Faith is the first requirement for justification but it entails 'all the obedience which the Gospel requires' and 'all the works of Christian piety' (1, pp. 64, 22). But faith is not the instrumental cause of justification, because justification is the work of God not humans. Faith excludes merit. However, 'by a figurative, but not an improper method of speaking' we may say that we are justified by faith alone. 'This expression is by all means to be kept, because it is best suited to express that grace and mercy of God by which, for Christ's sake, we are justified, and so entirely to remove all human merits from the work of justification' (1, pp. 68, 206). Bull follows the Thirty-nine Articles and the Homilies (both of which he appeals to extensively), the Augsburg Confession and other Reformation confessions, in holding that justification consists in forgiveness of sins rather than any imputation of Christ's righteousness (1, pp. 71ff.). He thus avoids Catholic strictures against Protestant teaching as a 'legal fiction' and escapes from medieval notions, perpetuated in Protestant theology, of the transfer of merit. Bull's whole discussion breathes the spirit of evangelical fervour and praise of divine grace. There is no moralistic harshness here.

Herbert Thorndike (1598–1672) would be a better example of a moralistic and legalistic approach, but Thorndike muddies the waters by using 'justification' as equivalent to 'salvation' (3.i, *passim*).

Daniel Waterland (1683–1740), who like Paley, Manning and Hare in the nineteenth century, combined the office of archdeacon with the vocation of a scholar, is our last representative of the 'holy living' school of eighteenth-century Anglican divines. We Protestants, Waterland insists, uphold the forensic sense of justification — and he calls Andrewes, Field and Bull to witness. The sanctifying influence of the Holy Spirit is necessarily presupposed in justification (as Hooker and Hammond had asserted) but is not to be identified or confused with it. While the efficient cause of justification is the Holy Spirit, applying the merits of Christ, the subordinate instruments — conveying justification to the believer — are word and sacraments, especially baptism. 'Baptism is, by Divine appointment, the ordinary instrument for conveying the grace of justification': as scripture, antiquity and the Anglican standards teach (9, pp. 429ff., 434, 450). Faith is the passive instrument of reception of justification. Obedience to the gospel is equally a condition or qualification for justification, but not a ground for it, for if justification could be achieved even by 'evangelical works', then 'Christ died in vain' (9, pp. 451f., 455). The Reformers contended for justification by faith alone in order to exclude merit. 'Thus came the doctrine of justification by faith alone, that is to say, by the alone merits and cross of Christ . . . to be a distinguishing principle of the Reformation' (9, p. 466).

As we have seen, the 'holy living' school places greater weight than the Jacobean and Caroline divines on repentance and obedience as human works stemming from the divine infusion of a principle of regenerate life, preparing us for justification. But the difference between the classical view and the 'holy living' school is not as great as is sometimes suggested (e.g. by C. F. Allison and McGrath). It remains a matter of emphasis. For the later divines justification is forensic and merit is disallowed; the distinction between justification and sanctification is preserved; repentance and obedience are the conditions not the causes of justification which is still said to be by faith. The Anglicanism of Bull and Waterland certainly still had a gospel to offer. The 'holy living' school was not a challenge to the consensus but a shift of emphasis within it.

It is John Henry Newman (1801–90) who in justification, as in ecclesiology (Avis, *Anglicanism*, ch. 14), delivered the most serious challenge to a consensus that included all shades of churchmanship. Newman's *Lectures on Justification* of 1838 have been described as 'perhaps the chief theological document of the Oxford Movement, the most important attempt to find the theological expression of its piety' (Brilioth, p. 282) and as 'the most important contribution to dogmatic theology to have come from the Tractarian school' (Reardon, p. 116). The book is indeed important, both for the theory of justification it advances and for the evidence it provides of Newman's view of the Reformation. But, as a contribution to dogmatics, it is weakened by rhetoric and caricature.

Newman tells us in the *Apologia* that the treatise on justification was aimed at 'the Lutheran dictum that justification by faith only was the cardinal doctrine of Christianity' (p. 150) — the article of a standing or falling Church. The lectures attempted a synthesis or middle way, claiming support from Melanchthon. 'I thought that the Anglican church followed Melanchthon and that in consequence between Rome and Anglicanism . . . there was no real intellectual difference on this point' (ibid.). Here Newman is being either disingenuous or astonishingly naïve.

Newman begins by observing that there are two views of justification found in Anglican theology: by faith and by obedience.

These are not incompatible unless developed into a system. The systems are the Protestant and Roman doctrines respectively. Neither of these can find room for an acceptable view of good works: either they introduce the idea of merit, or they tend (according to Newman, that is) to disparage works as prejudicial to salvation (*Justification*, pp. 1f.). It was on this human aspect that Newman intended to concentrate: 'I wished to fill up a ditch, the work of man' (*Apologia*, p. 150). At this point Newman summarizes the evangelical doctrine fairly: faith justifies 'not as being lively or fruitful, though this is an inseparable property of it, but as apprehending Christ, which is its essence' (*Justification*, p. 17). But he parts company with evangelical theology when he argues that the distinction between justification and sanctification is unscriptural, 'not in idea only but in fact' (ibid., pp. 44f.). Newman fails to realize that for Protestants the two are separated in idea only, not in fact.

Newman goes on to parody the Protestant doctrine of imputed righteousness, as though it exhausted the meaning of redemption:

> That the scheme of salvation should be one of names and understandings; that we should be but said to be just, said to have a righteousness, said to please God, said to earn a reward, said to be saved by works; that the great disease of our nature should remain unstaunched . . . all this would of course be a matter of faith if scripture declared it; but when merely propounded fifteen centuries after Christ came it has no claims upon us. (*Justification*, p. 62)

Newman's tilting at windmills has got into full swing; now there is no stopping him.

> Away then with this modern, this private, this arbitrary, this unscriptural system, which promising liberty conspires against it; which abolishes sacraments to introduce barren and dead ordinances; and for the real participation of Christ and justification through his Spirit, would at the very marriage feast feed us on shells and husks who hunger and thirst after righteousness. (*Justification*, p. 63)

Luther's is a 'new gospel', unheard of until three hundred years ago. A new gospel indeed! — Newman has just invented it himself.

The central thesis of the *Lectures* is that justification means 'making righteous' — though Newman is aware that the sense of the Greek New Testament is forensic, 'declaring righteous'. Newman resolves this discrepancy with the formula: 'in the abstract it is a counting righteous, in the concrete a making righteous' (*Justification*, pp. 71f.). The divine justifying word makes righteous because it is a creative word: 'the voice of the Lord calling us, calling us what we are not when it calls us, calling us what we then begin to be'.

Newman's is a doctrine of justification by anticipation: 'justification is at first what renewal could but be at last' (*Justification*, p. 81). Or as it is revealingly put in *Tract 90* (1841), faith justifies by anticipation, 'just as one might pay a labourer his hire before he began his work' (p. 13) (also Avis, 'The shaking of the Seven Hills').

Newman's doctrine of justification is a facet of his reaction to the Reformers. He has kept very little of their teaching. Although he employs the concept of the creative word of God, he fails to realize that it is authentically evangelical. While he is bound to accept that the New Testament doctrine of justification is essentially forensic, it clearly makes no appeal to him whatever and is not integrated into his thought. He is oblivious of the emphasis that the Reformers, especially Calvin, put on the believer's union with Christ. As a result he seriously misrepresents their teaching.

On the other hand, Newman has made marked concessions to the Roman or Tridentine position. As David Newsome has pointed out ('Justification and sanctification'), Newman will not allow the believer any assurance of salvation, such as might be provided by the doctrine of election. This would be quite incompatible with the moralistic rigour of the Oxford Movement, its profound sense of self-abasement and humility. Presumption was almost a mortal sin. As F. W. Faber wrote:

> O how I fear thee, living God,
>   With deepest, tenderest fears,
> And worship thee with trembling hope,
>   And penitential tears!

Furthermore, Newman's Freudian slips (unless his words were carefully chosen — in which case the point is reinforced) betray a complete abandonment of the evangelical understanding of justification. Phrases like 'paid as instalment', 'pay a labourer his hire', 'credit' and so on, give Newman's game away completely.

Newman had challenged the Anglican consensus on justification. Perhaps, like so many others, he had not appreciated the extent of that consensus. He had imagined that he could deploy Bull and other post-Restoration divines against earlier Anglican doctrine, but he had not realized the strength of the continuity between them. Newman did not understand his Anglican heritage. Moreover, his knowledge of the Reformation and its theology was negligible (see Avis, *Anglicanism*, ch. 14) and he twisted his sources, such as they were (McGrath, *Iustitia Dei*, 2, pp. 127ff.). To crown it all, Newman apparently failed to grasp the Tridentine doctrine also (ibid., p. 131). Not a very promising basis on which to attempt to construct a *via media*. His ultimate position was highly contorted and, characteristically, riddled with sophistry. It did not carry conviction.

Newman's challenge was refuted by F. D. Maurice (1805–72), a rare example of true insight into the world of Luther's theology whose influence permeated the liberal catholicism of the late nineteenth-century Anglican renaissance and led to a juster appreciation of the Reformation and its *articulus stantis* in the work of F. J. A. Hort, Henry Scott Holland, Charles Gore and ultimately Michael Ramsey. I have presented Maurice's interpretation of Luther and justification in *Anglicanism* (ch. 16), and Gore's doctrine of justification in *Gore* (pp. 34ff.). So here let Henry Scott Holland (1847–1918) speak as unquestionably the most eloquent representative of Anglican liberal catholicism.

Scott Holland was a soul friend of Charles Gore and contributed an essay on faith to the volume edited by Gore in 1889 *Lux Mundi*. In this essay Holland presents faith as the bond between humanity and its creator: 'it is an apprehensive motion of the living spirit, by which it intensifies its touch on God; it is an instinct of surrender . . . it is an affection of the will, by which it presses up against God, and drinks in divine vitality with quickened receptivity'. Though fundamentally trust not love, the moral will, the affections and love itself are its closest allies. It is a personal response to a Person and involves the whole of our human lives (pp. 11f., 23).

In the sermon 'The Law of Forgiveness' Holland applies these ideas to justification. The initiative is all with the grace of God: 'God must begin if ever we are to be rescued. Here is the very key of Christian theology, and the very core of Christian faith.' The evangelical note could hardly be clearer: 'Nothing of our own enters into the primary movement of our justification. No goodness at all of ours drew out a response from the cooperating favour of God. . . . He must forgive, before we have ceased to sin; he must justify, while still we lie guilty.' Holland admits that his language here recalls a popular theology that by isolating this emphasis has rendered it 'grotesque, unreal, deceptive — yes, and morally perilous'. But the concepts themselves are not to blame, only their isolation from complementary truths. The principle of justification by faith alone retains its validity as 'the assertion of our absolute exclusion from the creative act by which God acquits us; in that act we have no more part or lot than in the act of our first begetting. God forgives us without our helping him. We are justified, we are acquitted for and by nothing at all of our own, not even by our faith.'

The spirit of this sermon has far more in common with Maurice than with Newman, but at this point Holland turns to Newman's notions of God's creative word (not that this is Newman's prerogative, but perhaps Holland found it there) and the anticipatory nature of justification, but without Newman's overtones of commercial transactions and the Protestant work ethic, and set, moreover, within the splendid evangelical ethos that Holland has created by his exposition of prevenient grace.

> The act by which God forgives, carries with it, out of heaven, the power to work the change in us, which will justify God in forgiving. God's forgiveness goes out from him in such a form that it makes us, it enables us, it obliges us, to become that which we should be if we deserved to be forgiven. God the Father forgives us by anticipating that which will follow on his forgiveness.

Scott Holland has not sacrificed Newman's moral seriousness, but with it he has preserved the sense of joy and liberation which is authentic to the gospel and which marks all Holland's work. Finally, there is a certain almost metaphysical grandeur about his vision of a gracious God. 'Just as a secret act of God's original energy underlies all our natural life — one act, prevenient, enduring, hidden — so a secret act of forgiveness, original, enduring, prevenient, underlies all our regenerate life' (Holland, pp. 220–5).

In the teaching of a succession of Anglican theologians within the 'catholic' wing of the Church of England, the equilibrium in the doctrine of justification was regained and has not subsequently been lost.

In conclusion, we need to ask whether the new ecumenical consensus on justification, as expressed in the ARCIC II report *Salvation and the Church* is consistent with the Anglican tradition. Some Anglicans will want to measure that agreement against Luther or Calvin. They will not find much to complain about. But as Anglican participants in the ecumenical process we have to measure it not against the continental Reformers (who have their own distinctive emphases anyway), but against our Anglican formularies and our classical Anglican divines.

McGrath has stressed that the Tridentine doctrine of justification was by no means monolithic. A variety of views stemming from the medieval schools was tolerated. The same evidently applies to Anglicanism. If we acknowledge the reticence of our formularies and the richness of our theological heritage, we are bound to make room for a latitude of interpretation, though a continuing consensus on essentials can be discerned. An ecumenical statement on justification (or any other doctrinal topic for that matter) will not attempt a definitive doctrine, but will seek common ground, rule out deviations unacceptable to both sides and suggest areas where further work remains to be done. This *Salvation and the Church* does adequately.

However, as we have seen, a number of unanswered questions remain. For one thing, it is not at all clear that *Salvation and the*

Church is wholly reconcilable with Trent. The Roman magisterium will have to be persuaded to permit a perhaps unprecedented degree of latitude of interpretation of dogma before it can acknowledge the report as consistent with binding tradition. Then there remain questions concerning indulgences, the treasury of merits, obligatory penance, and the implications of justification for the categories of mortal and venial sins. Obviously this agreement does not go all the way in exploring justification. True, it cannot cover everything, but it did not have to be so slight and the commission could have worked on this for longer. It is a matter of judgement as to where was the right place to call a halt for the time being. But some evangelical Anglicans may feel that the report does not go far enough and lacks precision. In so saying they may be forgetting that there exists a diversity of views on justification within the Anglican tradition, yet one that presents no bar to communion. Surely Luther pointed us in the right direction when he consistently maintained that 'one thing was needful' and that if you got justification right, other matters would fall into place eventually.

The great ecumenical visionary and statesman — later Archbishop — William Wake, writing in reply to Bossuet three hundred years before ARCIC II, suggested that if points of terminology between the Anglican and the Roman Catholic doctrines of justification were clarified — particularly the distinction between justification and sanctification — agreement on this fundamental doctrine (though not on all the practical ramifications of it) would be close, and it would become apparent that (as Hooker had earlier perceived) both communions held the foundation of the faith in common (p. 21). *Salvation and the Church* at last brings that agreement significantly closer.

8

Communion
in the Spirit?

Holy Spirit creates communion

It is surely no accident that the only mention of *koinonia* in the story of the infant Church in the Acts of the Apostles follows immediately after Pentecost (Acts 2.42). The Holy Spirit is the source of communion between Christians. But the Spirit creates communion simply because that communion is ultimately a shared participation in (the) Holy Spirit.

Paul speaks of *koinonia* in the Spirit in two places. In 2 Corinthians 13.14 we have the trinitarian formula 'The grace': 'The grace of the Lord Jesus Christ and the love of God and the *koinonia* of the Holy Spirit be with you all'. And in Philippians 2.1 Paul appeals to that '*koinonia* of the Spirit' (*koinonia pneumatos*) that belongs to the common life, as the ground of unity between Christians. Commentators are divided on whether in these two texts *koinonia . . . pneumatos* should be interpreted 'communion or fellowship *imparted* by the Holy Spirit' (taking it as a subjective genitive) or 'communion or participation in the Holy Spirit' (taking it as an objective genitive). If Campbell is to be followed, and the primary and only common meaning of *koinonia* is participation along with others in something, then we must take these texts in the second sense, namely, 'communion or participation in the Holy Spirit' (so Campbell, pp. 25ff.; Barrett, *BNTC*, p. 344; Martin, *NCBC*, pp. 86f.; Thornton, pp. 69ff.; but cf. Congar, 1, p. 33; Schweizer, *TDNT*, 6, p. 434; Hauk, *TDNT*, 3, p. 807; Bruce, *NCBC*, p. 255). However, the niceties of translation are somewhat hypothetical since the meaning is substantially the same in either case: there can only be communion between Christians if there is already a common sharing in the Holy Spirit (Beare, *BNTC*, p. 71). But the objective genitive ('participation in (the) Holy Spirit') is confirmed by analogy with Hebrews 6.4: 'partakers (*metochous*) of the Holy Spirit'.

Our communion with one another as Christians is not merely on the basis of agreement in theology (the galloping pluralism of contemporary global Christianity is making that increasingly unattainable). It derives ultimately from sharing in a common gift. It is the gift of the Spirit that creates and brings about the Christian community. As Congar puts it, the Holy Spirit 'realizes the Christian mystery' (2, p. 68). Congar reminds us that the medieval schoolmen interpreted the third article of the creed, 'I believe in the Holy Spirit', to mean, 'I believe in the Holy Spirit as the one who gives life to the Church and makes her one, holy, catholic and apostolic' (2, p. 5 and ch. 2).

The Orthodox theologian John Zizioulas has stressed that it is the Holy Spirit who constitutes the Church as the body of Christ. In such a corporately conceived Christology, Christ is no mere individual but a transpersonal reality, a representative persona, anointed by the Spirit of God on behalf of all his people. For Zizioulas the Church is a pneumatological reality. The Holy Spirit is not so much 'the go-between God' (to cite John V. Taylor's suggestive phrase) as the present realization of Christ as the Church. Zizioulas writes:

> Here the Holy Spirit is not one who aids in bridging the distance between Christ and ourselves, but he is the person of the Trinity who actively realizes in history that which we call Christ, this absolutely relational entity, our Saviour. . . . All separation between Christology and ecclesiology vanishes in the Spirit. (*Being*, pp. 110f.)

I have suggested that John V. Taylor's phrase for the Holy Spirit — 'the go-between God' — perhaps does less than justice to the truth and that the Spirit is not merely located in between but also constitutes the reality and substance of divine life in the Church on earth. Nevertheless, we may be deeply grateful for the reminder Taylor gives us that it is the role of the Spirit to create new relationships and interactions, to reveal new insights and open up fresh possibilities. This applies both to the human and the divine Spirit. As Taylor puts it:

> My spirit . . . resides only in my relatedness to some other. Spirit is that which lies between, making both separateness and conjunction real. It generates a certain quality of charged intensity which from time to time marks every man's relationship with the world around him and with whatever reality lies within and behind that world. (p. 8)

At the heart of a theology of communion there lies a profound apprehension of the relational nature of all reality and a recognition that coming together, conjunction, 'conjugality', is a condition of life, growth and fruitfulness. Separation is sterile. In isolation we soon cease to be: only the shell of existence remains. 'We must love one another or die' (Auden). John Zizioulas has helped us to dig deeper foundations for ecumenical theology in the personalist anthropology of the Orthodox tradition. In his *Being as Communion* he has claimed as the legacy of Greek patristic thought the principle that 'there is no being without communion' and that nothing exists as 'an individual'

(p. 18). In the light of this axiom Zizioulas has sketched a brilliant reconstruction of ecclesiology, focused in the eucharist, which has radical implications for traditional Orthodox absolutism and exclusivism (cf. McPartlan; R. Williams; Lossky, pp. 121ff. 166f., 176).

However, the personalism that underlies the present work is of the homegrown variety and as a result is perhaps a little less exotic and less metaphysically ambitious. It is derived from the ethical personalism of John Oman and John Macmurray and the holism of Michael Polanyi. Macmurray wrote in the second series of his Gifford Lectures, *Persons in Relation*: 'there can be no man until there are at least two men in communication . . . the self exists only in dynamic relation with the other . . . persons are constituted by their mutual relation to one another' (pp. 12, 17). Behind Macmurray's ethical personalism lies the mystical personalism of Martin Buber's seminal *I and Thou* (1923). For Buber there is no such thing as discrete existence. 'In the beginning is relation.' There is no 'I' in itself; the I–Thou relation precedes 'I'. It also points beyond itself to its transcendent source: 'Every particular *Thou* is a glimpse through to the eternal *Thou*'. To relation belongs the genesis of spirit: 'Spirit is not in the *I* but between *I* and *Thou*' (pp. 18, 4, 22, 75, 39). Christian trinitarian theology takes this further.

In our reaching out to communion with each other as Christians of separated traditions we are actually being caught up into the transcendent dynamics of the trinitarian nature of God. We begin to participate in our poor human way in a drama that far exceeds our grasp. As T. F. Torrance (himself influenced by all the sources I have mentioned) has written:

> Within the Christian doctrine of God as three persons in one being, the concept of the Holy Spirit became intensely personal. The Holy Spirit is the sovereign divine subject, the creative, lifegiving personal presence of God who addresses man in his word, actualizing knowledge of God within man and creating in him the capacity to respond as a rational subject and agent to himself. It is through this inter-personal mode of his Presence to him that the Spirit brings man's human relations to their true end and fulfilment in God, for coming from the inner communion of love in the Holy Trinity he effects communion between man and God in love, that is, in the love that God himself *is*. ('The goodness and dignity of man', pp. 319f.)

The love that constitutes the divine life is echoed and emulated in human relations when 'the Holy Spirit dwells in our hearts and floods them with the love of God which he himself is, so that as he is the bond of oneness in the Holy Trinity, he may also be the bond of oneness and love and thus of intensely inter-personal relations among us'. In accord with our theme in this book, Torrance adds: 'It is thus that in our contingent frail human nature we may even be "partakers of the divine nature" as through the communion of the Holy Spirit we are allowed to share in the very love that God himself is' (ibid.).

Now perhaps we see why the Pauline author of Ephesians urges the Christians of Ephesus to 'maintain the unity of the Spirit in the bond of peace' (4.3). Here the NEB rendering 'the unity which the Spirit gives', taking *pneumatos* as a subjective genitive, destroys the suggestive ambiguity of the Greek which we could bring out by the paraphrase: 'the unity that you have by your shared participation in the Spirit'. The Holy Spirit, which is the bond of unity in the trinitarian life of God, is also and by virtue of that fact, the source of the unity of the body of Christ. This conception surely underlies the use of the same word unity (*henotes*) — its only other occurrence in the New Testament — in v. 13 of the same chapter. The gifts of ministry that the ascended Christ has bestowed upon his Church are 'for building up the body of Christ, until we all attain to the *unity* of the faith and of the knowledge of the Son of God, to mature manhood, to the measure of the stature of the fullness of Christ' (Ephesians 4.12f.). Though the Holy Spirit is not mentioned in this passage, s/he it is, according to the New Testament, who constitutes the body of Christ and brings to realization the Christological reality of the Church. Our communion in the Holy Spirit is, as Alasdair Heron has finely put it, 'participation in a movement of communication, recognition and response issuing from the heart of God himself' (p. 49).

The gift of the Spirit is the sole test of communion

This thesis is borrowed from the title of an essay by Roland Allen in his book *The Ministry of the Spirit* (1960). Allen describes the crisis that faced the early Church when it had to decide whether, and on what conditions, Gentiles were to be admitted to the Church. Was the Torah to be set aside? Was circumcision to be waived? Was baptism the only requirement? Would this lead to Gentile uncleanness in the household of God? It was a crisis of acceptance and of communion. How was it resolved? Allen replies: 'By one fact: God gave them the Holy Spirit' (p. 56).

Peter asked in the house of Cornelius: 'Can anyone forbid water for baptizing these people who have received the Holy Spirit just as we have?' When required by the apostles in Jerusalem to justify his action, he replied: 'If then God gave the same gift to them as he gave to us when we believed in the Lord Jesus Christ, who was I that I could withstand God?' (Acts 10.47; 11.17). Allen draws the conclusion:

> The gift of the Holy Ghost is thus seen to be the one necessity for communion. If the Holy Ghost is given, those to whom he is given are

certainly accepted in Christ by God. All who receive the Spirit are in reality and truth one. They are united by the strongest and most intimate of all ties. They are all united to Christ by his Spirit and therefore they are all united to one another. Men may separate them, systems may part them . . . but if they share the one Spirit, they are one. (p. 57)

Who are those who enjoy a participation in the Holy Spirit that forms the ground of their communion with one another? Are they perhaps, as some Pentecostalists and charismatics would have us believe, those who have received the 'baptism of the Holy Spirit' as a 'second blessing', subsequent to Christian initiation? Or are they, on the other hand, as some varieties of 'catholic' theology insist, those who have received the seal of the Spirit by confirmation at the hands of a bishop in the 'apostolic succession'?

The answer of the New Testament is unequivocal. Every Christian participates in the Holy Spirit by virtue of his or her baptism. Everyone who has faith in Christ has the Spirit of Christ and that Spirit was first given in baptism. The New Testament does not entertain anywhere the notion of a Christian believer without the indwelling Spirit. A brief tour of references to the gift of the Spirit should establish this conclusively.

All who are Christ's have the Spirit   Paul puts this negatively: 'Any one who does not have the Spirit of Christ does not belong to him' (Romans 8.9b); and positively: 'All who are led by the Spirit of God are sons of God' (ibid., 14). Sonship through Christ carries with it the Spirit of adoption: 'because you are sons, God has sent the Spirit of his Son into our hearts, crying "Abba! Father!" ' (Galatians 4.6). Our reconciliation, bringing the confidence to draw near to God, is *through* Christ and *in* the Spirit: 'Through him we . . . have access in one Spirit to the Father' (Ephesians 2.18).

All the baptized have the Spirit   As Peter promised on the Day of Pentecost to all who would repent and be baptized: 'You shall receive the gift of the Holy Spirit' (Acts 2.38). Paul cannot conceive of anyone, having been baptized, missing out on the gift of the Spirit: 'By one Spirit we were *all* baptized into one body . . . and *all* were made to drink of one Spirit' (1 Corinthians 12.13). Clearly referring to baptism, Paul links our justification with the work of the Holy Spirit: 'You were washed, you were sanctified, you were justified in the name of the Lord Jesus Christ and in the Spirit of our God' (1 Corinthians 6.11). Using what later became almost a technical term for baptism — enlightenment — the author of the Hebrews speaks of 'those who have once been enlightened, who have tasted the heavenly gift, and have become partakers of the Holy Spirit, and have tasted the goodness of the word of God and the powers of the age to come' (6.4f.). Romans

5.5 does not on the face of it carry any reference to baptism: 'God's love has been poured into our hearts through the Holy Spirit which has been given to us'; but by the analogy with 1 Corinthians 6.11 and Galatians 4.6 we see that the decisive past event to which Paul refers can only be baptism; we have here an example of what Thornton calls the 'baptismal aorist' (p. 88). Similarly, the 'sealing' with the Spirit, which is also described in terms suggestive of a decisive action in the past (2 Corinthians 1.22; Ephesians 1.13; 4.30) has been shown conclusively by Lampe in *The Seal of the Spirit* to refer to Christian initiation in baptism. By the second century 'sealing' was a synonym for baptism (Flemington, p. 60). Finally, two presumably late works of the New Testament make an unequivocal identification of baptism and the Spirit: the fourth gospel speaks of new birth through water and the Spirit (3.5) and Titus links 'the washing of regeneration and renewal in the Holy Spirit' (3.5).

The indwelling Christ and the indwelling Spirit are interchangeable Just as Paul can speak of Christians dwelling 'in Christ' (*en Christo*: 2 Corinthians 5.17) or 'in the Spirit' (*en pneumati*: Romans 8.9a), so too he speaks indifferently of Christ or the Spirit indwelling believers: 'if Christ is in you . . . if the Spirit of him who raised Jesus from the dead dwells in you . . . his Spirit which dwells in you' (Romans 8.9–11). Thus to have Christ is to have the Spirit. To distinguish is almost meaningless, for the Spirit is the Spirit of Christ (Romans 8.9b). Indeed in 2 Corinthians 3.14–18, Paul goes further, identifying Christ and the Spirit. Paul argues, first, that only through Christ is the veil that conceals the glory of God taken away (because that glory shines in the face of Christ); second, that when one turns to 'the Lord' it is taken away; and third, that 'the Lord' (*kurios*) is none other than the Spirit; finally he adds, in case there could be any doubt: 'this comes from the Lord (who is) the Spirit'. Now admittedly Paul did not normally think in syllogisms, and he is not afraid to mix his metaphors. But it seems to be undeniable that in this passage Paul identifies Christ and the Spirit, if not absolutely, at least to all practical intents and purposes.

In his study *Baptism in the Holy Spirit* James Dunn defends the thesis that:

> For the writers of the New Testament the baptism in or gift of the Spirit was part of the event (or process) of becoming a Christian, together with the effective proclamation of the gospel, belief in (*eis*) Jesus as Lord, and water-baptism in the name of the Lord Jesus; that it was the chief element in conversion–initiation, so that only those who had thus received the Spirit could be called Christians; that the reception of the Spirit was a very definite and often dramatic experience, the decisive and climactic experience in conversion–initiation. (p.4)

Without wishing to endorse all Dunn's conclusions in that book, it is gratifying to be able to deploy his central thesis in support of my argument that in the New Testament every baptized Christian enjoys the gift of the Spirit. I am assuming that the other conditions mentioned by Dunn, reception of the gospel message and faith in Christ, together with repentance (which Dunn does not mention here) have also to be fulfilled before individuals can be regarded as professing Christians. In the New Testament the gift of the Spirit and the fact of baptism are two sides of the same coin.

In conclusion, then: prior to and more important than the *gifts* of the Spirit, that seem to mark off Pentecostalists and charismatics from the staider mainstream of the Christian Church, stands the *gift* of the Spirit. The communion of Christians rests upon a shared experience and reality — the gift of the Spirit of Christ.

Holy Spirit forms the character of Christ in the Church

In our quest for a deeper understanding of the Holy Spirit we naturally turn first to what the Bible teaches. But we have to acknowledge that we look in vain for a complete and coherent doctrine of the Holy Spirit in the New Testament. The emphasis there is on the manifestations of the Spirit. In the New Testament the Spirit's presence is manifested in two distinct, but related ways: the *fruits* of the Spirit and in the *gifts* of the Spirit.

The *fruits* of the Spirit are the personal moral qualities of 'love, joy, peace, patience, kindness, goodness, faithfulness, gentleness, self-control' (Galatians 5.22–23). They are attributes of Christian character and should also therefore characterize the Church as a community. They are contrasted by St Paul with the works or fruits of the flesh; these are also attributes of a certain type of moral character (or perhaps rather, lack of it): 'fornication, impurity, licentiousness, idolatry, sorcery, enmity, strife, jealousy, anger, selfishness, dissension, party spirit, envy, drunkenness, carousing, and the like' (Galatians 5.19–21). The fruits of the Spirit comprise a catalogue of the moral qualities that make up the character of Christ as this is portrayed in the gospel traditions and reflected on in the epistles. For instance, the anatomy of charity in 1 Corinthians 13 with its picture of a suffering, gentle, indestructible love, reminds us irresistibly of the figure of the gospels and must surely have been shaped by Paul's reflection on the traditions he had received concerning 'the Son of God, who loved me and gave himself for me' (Galatians 2.20).

It is the Spirit of Jesus himself that indwells the believer and the community into which he or she is incorporated by baptism. For the body into which we were baptized by the one Spirit is the body of

Christ, or even simply 'Christ' (1 Corinthians 12.12, 13, 27). Life in the Spirit and in the Body is progressively shaped by conformity, through obedience and suffering, to the image and likeness of Jesus Christ — or as we might say, to his moral character. As we behold the glory of the Lord in the Gospel we are 'changed into his likeness from one degree of glory to another'. 'All this', adds Paul, 'comes from the Lord who is the Spirit' (2 Corinthians 3.18). The epistle to the Colossians makes the same point, though without mentioning the Holy Spirit, when it exhorts those who have been raised with Christ to set their minds on things that are above, where Christ is throned in glory, and not on things that are of the earth. The contrast is made in terms of moral character. Believers are to put to death, in union with Christ's cross, the earthly residue of fornication, impurity, passion, evil desire, covetousness, anger, wrath, malice, slander, foul talk and lies. They are to live in the power of the new nature which is theirs through their baptismal union with Christ's resurrection, and which is being continually renewed in knowledge after the image of its creator. This new nature shows forth the moral qualities of compassion, kindness, lowliness, meekness, patience, forbearance, forgiveness, love, peaceableness and thankfulness. Here the figure of the gospel traditions is surely not far away. Christians are being renewed in the image of Christ who is himself the image of the invisible God (Colossians 3.1–17; 1.15).

It is clear that the fruits of the Spirit are the outward signs, apparent in Christian character, of a whole new quality of existence that Christians are called to experience through their baptismal incorporation into the risen Body of Christ, the Church, the place where the Spirit of Jesus continues his work of perfecting Christlikeness in the believer. Incorporation into the saving events of the cross and resurrection, and incorporation into the Body of Christ, the living fellowship of the Spirit, are one and the same act. The generous, sacrificial love (*agape*) that provided the momentum of Jesus Christ's journey to the cross, is the bond of fellowship within his risen Body and the primary mark of the indwelling presence of the Spirit.

This brief account of the fruits of the Spirit suggests two areas for further reflection. First, all this may seem a far cry from the actual behaviour of most Christians, in church history and today. Many of us are not conspicuously successful at exhibiting such Christlike qualities. Though this uncomfortable fact does not diminish the strength and urgency of the New Testament's exhortation to us to 'become what we are' in Christ, it does set a humbling paradox at the centre of anything we may want to say about the power of the Spirit in the Church. We shall find that this applies as much to spiritual *gifts* as to spiritual *fruits*.

Second, we are bound to acknowledge that the personal moral qualities that mark the Christian character, as it brings forth the fruits of the Spirit, are not exclusive to Christians. The Church does not have a monopoly of the virtues. Often it is put to shame by those of other faiths or none. There is nothing uniquely Christian about love, joy, peace, patience, kindness, goodness, faithfulness, gentleness and self-control (Galatians 5.22) — though for Christians these virtues are given concrete reality in the character of Christ where they are held to reveal the very character of God. Research and discussion continues over whether *agape* was, as is sometimes claimed, a truly innovatory conception of love that had to be invented by the first Christians to describe the matchless quality of Christ's compassion (cf. Avis, *Eros*, chs 15 and 16). But in general it is clear that the moral virtues that the New Testament identifies as the fruits of the Spirit are the very moral virtues that philosophers ancient and modern, moralists, rabbis and other religious teachers have inculcated as the ideal for all humanity. Of course humanity in the mass has disastrously failed to achieve the consistent practice of these virtues — and this underlines the Christian claim for the need for divine assistance to live the risen life. But whether humanity in general has been less successful in following the ideals held out by its best teachers than the Church has in embodying the character of Christ is a moot point.

Am I undermining the uniqueness of the incarnation and its consequences by claiming that the Christian virtues coincide with non-Christian ideals? The virtual identity of Christlike qualities with time-honoured moral ideals may be disturbing to those Christians who tend to operate with a dualistic picture of God and the world — who stress the irreparable alienation of humankind from God, the catastrophic consequences of the 'Fall', the depravity of human nature, the pride of human reason, the idolatrous character of human cultural achievement, and the embattled state of the Church as a tiny remnant fighting a rearguard action against overwhelming hostile forces. Indeed that is a scenario that almost forces itself upon us at certain dark moments of history, and perhaps above all in our present century when it seems that unprecedented evil has been unleashed upon the world.

But the continuity between Christian qualities graced by the Spirit of Jesus and the moral ideals of philosophers and religious teachers throughout the ages, will commend itself to those Christians who belong within a tradition that is continually mindful of the biblical teaching that humanity is created in the image of God, that the light which came into the world uniquely in the incarnation is the same light that enlightens every human creature, that the Spirit moves where it wills, that the truth of God is apparent in the visible world, that God has not left himself without witness at any time, and that he is not far from any one of us for in him we live and move and have our being (Genesis 1.26f.; John 1.9; 3.8; Romans 1.19f.; Acts 14.17; 17.27f.). This is the tradition that has held on to the insight that divine grace does not abolish human nature but perfects it. St Thomas Aquinas, who articulates this principle in its classical form, specifically relates it to the moral virtues and Christian character when he says that just as grace does not do away with nature but brings it to perfection, so the natural loving inclination yields to Christian charity (*ST*, Ia, 1.8.2).

Thus it becomes clear that the fruits of the Spirit should be understood, not as unprecedented attributes sent down from above to be greeted with blank incomprehension by an unbelieving world, but rather as created natural human endowments or potentialities, to be attributed to God's creative generosity wherever they are found, and capable of being evoked, nurtured and sustained, made concrete, shaped, and given identity by the Spirit of Jesus within the Body of Christ, to be accepted with grateful recognition as what we have always known, seen afar off, and longed to make our own. We shall shortly have to ask whether this principle of the consecration of created natural potentialities to Christian discipleship and to the glory of God does not also apply equally to spiritual *gifts*.

The New Testament epistles betray little knowledge of or interest in the earthly history or human characteristics of Jesus of Nazareth. This fact makes it all the more significant that they are powerfully orientated towards the realization of the *moral character* of Jesus in the Church through the Holy Spirit. Moule comments that the New Testament 'reflects an understanding of the Holy Spirit as essentially a mediator, in each individual, of the character of Christ' (p. 82). There is a Christological criterion for identifying the Spirit's presence and it is not mystical but moral. The Spirit is recognized as the power that transforms us into the image of Christ (2 Corinthians 3.18). As Dunn comments, the Spirit has taken on the character of Christ (*Jesus and the Spirit*, p. 322).

The kingdom of God is not concerned with external ritual distinctions ('food and drink') but with 'righteousness and peace and joy in the Holy Spirit' (Romans 14.17). Thornton asserts that the gospel 'secured a transformation of the relations between the sacred and the profane . . . from a physical to an ethical basis' (p. 17), though in this it represented the culmination of a long process of spiritual discrimination through the teaching of the canonical prophets and their rabbinic interpreters. The shift is reflected in the increasing dominance of the moral over the ceremonial aspect of ritual ablutions (*baptismoi*). Lampe insists that, though all Jewish baptisms were purificatory, the baptism of John was unique in its ethical significance

(*Seal*, p. 24). The language of Christian moral character in the epistles is imbued with baptismal imagery. Those who died to sin in baptism thereby became 'obedient from the heart to the standard of teaching' (Romans 6.17f.). Ephesians 5.8f. uses the language of baptismal enlightenment, adding: 'the fruit of light is found in all that is good and right and true'. In 1 Timothy 6.12–14 'Paul' addresses Timothy: 'you made the good confession . . . keep the commandment unstained'. 1 Peter 1–4 is probably a baptismal discourse and combined *kerygma* and *didache*, proclamation of the gospel and instruction in the Christian life. The baptismal confession of faith in the Lordship of Jesus Christ entailed accepting basic ethical obligations (Beasley-Murray, pp. 284ff.).

Congar concludes his survey of the New Testament references to the fruits of the Spirit with the reflection that they present us with an ideal portrait of the Christian who is peacefully and joyfully ready to welcome, and calmly and patiently open to love his or her fellows. They speak of a 'fragile imitation of Christ' who was gentle and lowly in heart (Matthew 11.29), given up to God and human need, 'free, trustful, demanding, merciful, recollected and open to all' (2, p. 138).

But what has the mission of the Spirit, to form the character of Christ in the Church, to do with the Church as a communion? The relevance lies in the paradox that the grace of the *Holy* Spirit is *commonly* shared. Just as in English the words 'communion' and 'common' are cognate, so in Greek *koinonia*, communion, is allied to *koinos*, common or unclean — the precise opposite of *hagios*, holy (Quick, *Doctrines*, p. 284). So, if the Old Testament concept of holiness means *separation*, the New Testament concept means, even more than ethics, *participation*. The moral character of Christ is imparted to the Church through communion in the Body of Christ.

Spiritual gifts are intended to serve Christian communion

We observed that in the New Testament, the presence of the Holy Spirit is manifested in two distinct but related ways: in the *fruits* of the Spirit and in the *gifts* of the Spirit. Now the *gifts* of the Spirit are those talents or special abilities that God gives to every individual believer for the common good. One of the earliest references to spiritual gifts occurs in Paul's first epistle to the Corinthians:

> To each is given the manifestation of the Spirit for the common good. To one is given through the Spirit the utterance of wisdom, and to another the utterance of knowledge according to the same Spirit, to another faith by the same Spirit, to another gifts of healing by the one Spirit, to another the working of miracles, to another prophecy, to another the ability to distinguish between spirits, to another various kinds of tongues, to another the interpretation of tongues. (1 Corinthians 12.7–10)

'All these', adds Paul, 'are inspired by one and the same Spirit, who apportions to each one individually as he wills' (v. 11). Several points are worth noting here.

First, Paul is stressing the *variety* of gifts that exist in the Christian community: 'There are varieties of gifts . . . there are varieties of service . . . there are varieties of working' (vv. 4–6). We should not expect all Christians to enjoy the same gifts. And there is absolutely no suggestion that lack of any particular gift implies lack of spiritual attainment: 'Do all work miracles? Do all possess gifts of healing? Do all speak with tongues? Do all interpret?' (vv. 29–30). The question is rhetorical: the implied answer is an emphatic No! Diversity of gifts is a further aspect of that Christian pluralism of which we are particularly conscious today.

Second, Paul is labouring the point that, however diverse the gifts, they are all bestowed by the *same Spirit*. His language is intended to drive home, beyond any possibility of misunderstanding, the truth that all gifts and talents, the ecstatic and the controlled, the dramatic and the humdrum, are equally the work of the Holy Spirit: 'The same Spirit . . . the same Lord . . . the same God who inspires them all in every one' (vv. 4–6). Paul is clearly attempting to forestall any suggestion that the Spirit might be given in greater measure to some who have certain gifts, and in lesser measure to others with certain other gifts. He leaves no scope for spiritual pride, but rather emphasizes that the weaker and humbler members, whose gifts may seem nothing to boast about, are all the more essential to the effective working of the Body of Christ, just as the 'unpresentable' parts of the human body are modestly concealed even though they have a particularly vital part to play in the healthy functioning of the whole body (vv. 14–16). The diversity of gifts springs from a common source.

Third, Paul appears to set the gifts in some sort of *hierarchy of value*. Though they are all bestowed by the same sovereign Spirit and are all equally vital for the life of the Church, it is good to aspire to the 'higher gifts'. 'God has appointed in the church', Paul writes, 'first apostles, second prophets, third teachers, then workers of miracles, then healers, helpers, adminstrators, speakers in various kinds of tongues' (v. 28). It is significant that while prophets are ranked before teachers, the latter take priority over miracle workers, just as helpers and administrators take precedence over speakers in tongues. There can be little doubt that Paul's words in these chapters 12–14 of 1 Corinthians are aimed at those who over-valued tongues: here Paul puts tongues 'at the bottom of the league'. Gifts are ranked according to their usefulness to the Church.

Fourth, Paul makes *no distinction* between the ecstatic (or as we might say, paranormal) gifts such as miracles, healings, tongues and interpretation, on the one hand, and the undramatic, mundane and everyday gifts such as helping and administering, on the other. This becomes even clearer in that other early discussion of spiritual gifts in Romans 12 where Paul lists prophecy, service, teaching, exhorting, contributing, giving aid and performing acts of mercy (vv. 6–8). Here, it seems, Paul is casting around the Christian community to see what was going on, and making sure that no one's contribution was overlooked. Today, however, it seems that we cannot avoid making a distinction between those gifts that appear to be natural human endowments and those that seem to demand a 'super-natural' explanation. We need to ask whether such a division is justified.

Tongues, prophecy and healing are all run of the mill topics in comparative anthropology. They are very far from being unique to charismatic Christians. Healing in particular, without conventional, Western medical means, is a universal phenomenon. Today there are a great many 'natural' healers — some Christians, some not — who have been led to discover a power within themselves — often apparently transmitted though the hands — that can release the innate healing resources of the human mind and body. The inescapable empirical fact that 'paranormal' gifts such as tongues, prophecy and healing are universal leads us to conclude that, like Christian moral virtues — the *fruits* of the Spirit — these *gifts* of the Spirit are created, God-given, natural endowments or potentialities, that can be activated or 'triggered' under certain conditions. Like other human abilities, they can be used for good or ill — consecrated to the glory of God and the well-being of others, or abused and exploited for self-glorification and domination. This assessment of the nature of spiritual gifts leads us to resist a direct identification between all charismatic phenomena and the work of the Holy Spirit. To make an impartial, discriminating and critical assessment of these phenomena is not to quench the Spirit or sit in judgement on the sovereign work of God. It also explains why many Christians can be profoundly thankful to God for the charismatic movement while others are deeply disturbed by certain aspects of it — the inculcation of credulity, the use of manipulative techniques verging on the hypnotic, and lack of verification and long-term assessment of results.

Charismatic Christians are caught up in the great contemporary movement to strengthen the bonds of communion between Christians of historically separated traditions. The charismatic movement has done much to break down those barriers. But Christian unity is all about deepening understanding within the context of unreserved acceptance. Do charismatics extend that acceptance to the staider mainstream traditions? Do they acknowledge that according to the New Testament every baptized believer has received the gift of the

Spirit? Do they really believe that the primary task of the Spirit is not to produce special effects and titillating experiences, puerile inducements for under-age Christians, but to form the character of Christ in the Church? Do they accept that the enjoyment of extraordinary spiritual gifts, far from setting charismatic Christians above their fellows, in fact underlines the truly human, universal character of religious expression and imposes an additional responsibility to use such gifts not for self-indulgence or self-aggrandizement, but for the glory of God in Christ and the well-being of his Church? Ultimately our communion as Christians is a communion in the Spirit. It would be profoundly ironical if charismatics themselves were to fail to rise to the challenge that the Spirit offers. But the contribution they can make to the vitality of the Church is too important for any of us to allow that to happen — and that is precisely why I am raising these rather searching questions.

Communion creates Holy Spirit

I have been arguing that communion between Christians is created by the Holy Spirit who indwells us. I now want to stand that on its head and put forward the proposition that communion actually creates (the) Holy Spirit. In making that paradoxical statement I do not want to be interpreted as challenging trinitarian orthodoxy which presents the Holy Spirit as one of three equal 'persons' of the godhead. Although this formulation cannot be found in the New Testament where Christ and the Spirit are almost interchangeable, and remains a contingent, historical, human interpretation, nevertheless I believe that it is morally (I do not say judicially) binding upon us and constitutes the inescapable framework of Christian doctrine. But it is highly symbolic and analogical and that gives ample scope for liberty of interpretation. So I am not venturing any metaphysical statement of trinitarian doctrine at all in putting forward the proposition that communion between Christians creates Holy Spirit.

In fact I believe that I am in tune with the emphasis of the New Testament. For the picture of the Spirit that emerges from the New Testament is a narrowly and intensely focused one. The Spirit is the Spirit of Jesus and dwells in his body the Church. The Spirit is always found indwelling believers, both individually and corporately. Speculation about the distinct 'personal' (hypostatic) existence of the Spirit in the godhead, or about the Spirit's wider 'cosmic' functions, is conspicuously absent (Moule, *The Holy Spirit*, p.19). There is much to be said — without inferring that it is all that can be said — for Schleiermacher's view that 'the expression "Holy Spirit" must be understood to mean the vital unity of the Christian fellowship . . . its common spirit' (p. 535).

I believe it is a great mistake — and a product of what Marx called 'false consciousness' — to assume that the Holy Spirit is a sort of substance or perhaps fluid that can be contained in certain (human) vessels, directed through particular (sacramental) channels, possessed, guaranteed, and deployed as a sort of force. I would rather think in personalist and dynamic terms of the Spirit emerging, being generated, coming about, being liberated, indeed being created.

There is that remarkable text in John 7.39: literally, 'Spirit was not yet, for Jesus was not yet glorified'. John does not mean that the Spirit did not exist, or that there was no Spirit, for he has already told of the Spirit resting upon Jesus (1.32f.) in unlimited fullness (3.34) and of the necessity of being born of the Spirit (3.5) and worshipping in the Spirit (4.23f.), of the Spirit giving life and being contained in or conveyed by the words of Jesus (6.63). To that extent, the translations that supply 'given' after 'Spirit was not yet' are no doubt bringing out the intention of the fourth evangelist, though doing so on minimal textual authority. John clearly means that the Spirit was not yet identified as the Spirit of the crucified and risen Jesus. Something had to happen before the Spirit of Jesus would be unleashed, become available, be made present. That sense of a void yet to be filled is brought out by letting the original stand in its stark mystery: 'Spirit was not yet . . .'.

The same suggestion of God's reality becoming manifest in our midst — brought about, called into being by the mutual love of Christians — is found in 1 John 4.12 (NEB): 'Though God has never been seen by any man, God himself dwells in us if we love one another; his love is brought to perfection within us'. Then John significantly adds: 'Here is the proof that we dwell in him and he dwells in us: he has imparted his Spirit to us' (v. 13). Our love for one another brings about God as Spirit in our midst — a reality that would not exist otherwise.

To take an Old Testament parallel: with its quaint and amusing picture of the oil of high priestly anointing running down from Aaron's head over his face and beard and down his neck, Psalm 133 suggests that loving fellowship is a condition of divine unction and God's blessing:

> Behold, how good and pleasant it is when brothers dwell in unity! It is like the precious oil upon the head, running down upon the beard, upon the beard of Aaron, running down on the collar of his robes. It is like the dew of Hermon, which falls on the mountains of Zion! For there the Lord has commanded the blessing, life for evermore.

So it proved on the Day of Pentecost: it was when the disciples 'were all with one accord in one place' (Acts 2.1) that the Spirit came.

The basic meaning of Holy Spirit is the presence or activity of God in the world (Moule, *The Holy Spirit*, p. 4). When the Psalmists contemplate God withdrawing his presence, they say, 'Take not thy Holy Spirit from me'; note the parallel: 'Cast me not away from thy presence . . .' (Psalm 51.11). Compare Psalm 139.7: 'Whither shall I go from thy Spirit? Or whither shall I flee from thy presence?' The prophet Haggai encourages the people to rebuild the temple: 'My Spirit abides among you; fear not' (Haggai 2.5). God's presence is not only protection and blessing but action and power: 'Not by might, nor by power, but by my Spirit, says the Lord of hosts' (Zechariah 4.6).

Spirit mediates between God and the world, deity and humanity, transcendence and immanence. Like 'word' and 'wisdom', 'Spirit' is a mediating word (Moule, *The Holy Spirit*, p. 7) and stands for divine–human interaction. As Lampe comments, these are all

> quasi-poetical words, expressive of a profoundly mysterious inner awareness of confrontation with transcendent personal grace, love, demand, judgement, forgiveness, and calling. In their original usage they are not metaphysical terms, analytically descriptive of the structure of deity itself; nor do they denote hypostatically existent mediators between God and the world. They refer, rather, to the human experience of being, as it were, reached out to and mysteriously touched and acted upon by transcendent deity. (*God as Spirit*, p. 37)

It is surely significant that spirit can be predicated of both God and humanity. In Hebrew and Greek, as well as English, 'the same word can denote the human spirit, that is man as a rational, feeling, willing, personality endowed with insight, wisdom and moral sensitivity, capable of responding to God, and also the creative and life-renewing power of God which is nothing less than his personal presence' (Lampe, ibid., p. 44). It is a commonplace that it is often impossible to tell whether a given reference to *ruach* or *pneuma* should be translated as spirit or Spirit. Which does the Psalmist intend when he says: 'Put a new and right *ruach* within me . . . and uphold me with a willing *ruach*' (Psalm 51.10b, 12b)? And the two senses overlap and almost merge in 1 Corinthians 2.10–13: the wisdom of God is what

> God has revealed to us through the *pneuma*. For the *pneuma* searches everything, even the depths of God. For what person knows a man's thoughts except the *pneuma* of the man which is in him? So also no one comprehends the thoughts of God except the *pneuma* of God. Now we have received not the *pneuma* of the world, but the *pneuma* which is from God, that we might understand the gifts bestowed on us by God. And we impart this in words not taught by human wisdom but taught by the *pneuma*, interpreting spiritual truths to those who possess the *pneuma*.

The ambiguity is even more intriguing where the Greek lacks the definite article. Commenting on this passage, Moule is bold to say: 'In revelation, Paul seems to say, the divine Spirit touches (or even coincides or coalesces with?) man's spirit' (*The Holy Spirit*, p. 10; cf. Lampe, *God as Spirit*, pp. 44ff.; cf. also Romans 8.26f.).

John V. Taylor is certainly on St Paul's wavelength when he writes: 'The spirit of man is that facility which enables each of us to be truly present to another. The Spirit of God is that power of communion which enables every other reality, and the God who is within and behind all realities, to be present to us' (p. 19). It would seem to follow that only if we are open to one another can we be open to God's Spirit, because spirit is the *milieu* in which God works. Taylor writes:

> If one is open towards God, one is open also to the beauty of the world, the truth of ideas, and the pain of disappointment and deformity. If one is closed up against being hurt, or blind towards one's fellow-men, one is inevitably shut off from God also. One cannot choose to be open in one direction and closed in another. Vision and vulnerability go together. (p. 19)

Our duty is clear: if we want to enjoy the grace of the Holy Spirit and taste the powers of the age to come, we must seek by all means available to us to enter into unreserved communion with our fellow Christians on the basis of total mutual acceptance and regard. This surely has something to say to charismatics who believe that they enjoy a special privilege regarding the endowment of the Spirit, but it speaks to all churches, for their greatest need is the vitality that the Spirit gives. Without it they are mere institutions, bureaucratic organizations, power-structures and property-owners, requiring the gifts of the faithful to keep them grinding along — resources that if they are not to be available to enable the Holy Spirit to work in the world through human channels could be better directed to some *truly* humanitarian purpose!

Am I advocating a form of Pelagianism — of human initiative that attempts to manipulate divine response — the only heresy, as Archbishop William Temple used to say, that was intrinsically damnable? No, beyond and behind all our human motivation is the sovereign work of the Holy Spirit, working in us to will and perform his good pleasure (Philippians 2.13). Even our faith is the gift of God's grace (Ephesians 2.8). But we should not presume upon it. You cannot control or predict the Spirit that blows where it wills (John 3.8). Our path of obedience is clear: to create the conditions that enable the Spirit to manifest God's gracious presence in our midst. Martin Buber wrote: 'We are waiting for a theophany about which we know nothing except its place, and that place is called community' (cf. Taylor, p. 16).

Bibliography

By author

Allchin, A. M. *Participation in God* (London: Darton, Longman & Todd, 1988).

Allen, R. *The Ministry of the Spirit* (London: World Dominion, 1960).

Allison, C. F. *The Rise of Moralism* (London: SPCK, 1966).

Allison, C. F. 'The pastoral and political implications of Trent on justification', *One in Christ*, **24** (1988), pp. 112–27.

Allison, D. C. *The End of the Ages has Come* (Edinburgh: T. & T. Clark, 1987).

Avis, P. D. L. 'The shaking of the Seven Hills', *Scottish Journal of Theology*, **32** (1979), pp. 439–55.

Avis, P. D. L. *The Church in the Theology of the Reformers* (London: Marshall Morgan and Scott, 1982).

Avis, P. D. L. 'Luther's theology of the Church', *Churchman*, **97** (1983), pp. 104–11.

Avis, P. D. L. *Ecumenical Theology and the Elusiveness of Doctrine* (London: SPCK, 1986; *Truth Beyond Words*, Cambridge, MA: Cowley, 1986).

Avis, P. D. L. *Foundations of Modern Historical Thought: From Machiavelli to Vico* (London: Croom Helm, 1986).

Avis, P. D. L. 'Reflections on ARCIC II', *Theology*, **90** (1987), pp. 451–9.

Avis. P. D. L. *Gore: Construction and Conflict* (Worthing: Churchman, 1988).

Avis, P. D. L. *Anglicanism and the Christian Church* (Edinburgh: T. & T. Clark; Minneapolis: Augsburg/Fortress, 1989).

Avis, P. D. L. *Eros and the Sacred* (London: SPCK, 1989; Wilton, CT: Morehouse, 1990).

Barrett, C. K. 'Shaliaḥ and Apostle' in E. Bammel, C. K. Barrett and W. D. Davies (eds) *Donum Gentilicium: New Testament Studies in Honour of David Daube* (Oxford: Clarendon, 1978).

Beasley-Murray, G. R. *Baptism in the New Testament* (London: Macmillan, 1962).

Bedale, S. 'The meaning of *kephalē* in the Pauline Epistles', *Journal of Theological Studies*, N.S. **5** (1954), pp. 211–15.

Bennett, G. V. *To the Church of England* (Worthing: Churchman, 1988).

Best, E. *One Body in Christ* (London: SPCK, 1955).

Beveridge, W. *The Doctrine of the Church of England*, 2nd edn (*Works*, LACT, vol. 7).

Bonhoeffer, D. *Sanctorum Communio* (London: Collins, 1963).

Børresen, K. E. *Subordination and Equivalence: The Nature and Role of Women in Augustine and Thomas Aquinas*, rev. edn (Washington, DC: University Press of America, 1981).

Bramhall, J. *A Just Vindication of the Church of England* (*Works*, LACT, vol. 1).

Brilioth, Y. *The Anglican Revival* (London, 1925).

Brinkman, B. R. *To the Lengths of God: Truth and the Ecumenical Age* (London: Sheed, 1988).

Brock, S. 'The priesthood of the baptized: Some Syriac perspectives', *Sobornost*, **9** (1987), pp. 14–22.

Buber, M. *I and Thou* (Edinburgh: T. & T. Clark; New York: Scribners, 1937).

Bull, G. *Harmonia Apostolica* (*Works*, 2nd edn, LACT).

Calvin, J. *Institutes of the Christian Religion*, trans. H. Beveridge (London: Clarke, n.d.).

Calvin, J. *Tracts and Treatises*, ed. T. F. Torrance (Grand Rapids, MI: Eerdmans, 1958).

Calvin, J. *Calvin's Commentaries: The First Epistle to the Corinthians*, trans. J. W. Fraser (Edinburgh: St Andrew, 1960).

Campbell, J. Y. *Three New Testament Studies* (Leiden: Brill, 1965).

Chadwick, H. 'Justification by faith: A perspective', *One in Christ*, **20** (1984), pp. 191–225.

Clebsch, W. A. *England's Earliest Protestants 1520–1535* (Westport, CT: Greenwood Press, 1980).

Clément, O. 'Orthodox ecclesiology as an ecclesiology of Communion', *One in Christ*, **4** (1970), pp. 101–22.

Congar, Y. *I Believe in the Holy Spirit* (3 vols; London: Geoffrey Chapman; New York: Seabury, 1983).

Cullmann, O. *Baptism in the New Testament* (London: SCM, 1950).

Davenant, J. *A Treatise on Justification*, trans. J. Allport (Dublin and Birmingham, 1844).

Davey, C. *Pioneer for Unity: Metrophanes Kritopoulos (1589–1639) and Relations between the Orthodox, Roman Catholic and Reformed Churches* (London: BCC, 1987).

de Lubac, H. *Catholicism* (London: Burns, Oates and Washbourne, 1949).

de Lubac, H. *Méditation sur l'Église* (3rd edn; Paris: Aubier, 1954).

Draper, J. (ed.) *Communion and Episcopacy* (Ripon College Cuddesdon, 1988).

Dulles, A. *Models of the Church* (New York: Doubleday, 1974).

Dunn, J. D. D. *Baptism in the Holy Spirit* (London: SCM, 1970).

Dunn, J. D. D. *Jesus and the Spirit* (London: SCM, 1975).

Evans, G. R. (ed.) *Christian Authority: Essays in Honour of Henry Chadwick* (Oxford: Clarendon, 1988).

Evans, R. F. *One and Holy: The Church in Latin Patristic Thought* (London: SPCK, 1972).

Field, R. *Of the Church* (Edinburgh, 1847).

Flannery, A. (ed.) *Vatican Council II: More Post-Conciliar Documents* (New York: Costello, 1982).

Flemington, W. F. *The New Testament Doctrine of Baptism* (London: SPCK, 1948).

Florovsky, G. 'The doctrine of the Church and the ecumenical problem', *Ecumenical Review*, **2** (1950), pp. 152–6.

Fouyas, M. *Orthodoxy, Roman Catholicism and Anglicanism* (London: OUP, 1972).

Forbes, W. *Considerationes Modestae et Pacificae: I. De Justificatione* (*Works*, LACT).

Gibbs, L.W. 'Richard Hooker's *via media* doctrine of justification', *Harvard Theological Review*, **74** (1981), pp. 211–20.

Gore, C. *The Church and the Ministry* (2nd edn; London: Murray, 1889).

Gore, C. (ed.) *Lux Mundi* (London: Murray, 1889).

Gundry, E. H. *Sōma in Biblical Theology* (Cambridge: CUP, 1976).

Hales, J. *On Schism* (London, 1700).

Hammond, H. *A Practical Catechism* (*Works*, LACT).

Hanson, A. T. *The Pioneer Ministry* (London: SCM, 1961).

Hanson, A. T. and R. P. C. *The Identity of the Church* (London: SCM, 1987).

Heron, A. I. C. *The Holy Spirit* (London: Marshall, Morgan & Scott, 1983).

Hill, E. *Ministry and Authority in the Catholic Church* (London: Geoffrey Chapman, 1988).

Hogan, R. M. and le Voir, J. M. *Faith for Today: The Teachings of Pope John Paul II* (New York: Doubleday, 1988; London: Collins, 1989).

Holland, H. S. *Creed and Character* (London, 1897).

Hooker, R. *Works*, ed. J. Keble (Oxford: Parker, 1845).

Hopko, T. (ed.) *Women and the Priesthood* (New York: St Vladimir's Seminary Press, 1983).

Hort, F. J. A. *The Christian Ecclesia* (London: Macmillan, 1914).

Hughes, J. J. *Absolutely Null and Utterly Void: The Papal Condemnation of Anglican Orders 1896* (London: Sheed and Ward, 1968).

Hume, B. *Towards a Civilization of Love* (London: Hodder, 1988).

Keble, J. 'The State in its relations with the Church', *British Critic*, **26** (1839), pp. 335–97.

Kelly, J. N. D. *Early Christian Creeds* (London: Longmans, 1950).

Khomyakov, A. S. 'On the Western confessions of faith' in A. Schmemann (ed.) *Ultimate Questions: An Anthology of Modern Russian Religious Thought* (London: Mowbray, 1977).

Küng, H. *Justification* (new edn; London: Burns & Oates, 1981).

Lampe, G. W. H. *The Seal of the Spirit* (London: Longmans, Green & Co., 1951).

Lampe, G. W. H. '*Baptisma* in the New Testament', *Scottish Journal of Theology*, **5** (1952), pp. 163–74.

Lampe, G. W. H. *God as Spirit* (Oxford: Clarendon, 1977).

Limouris, G. 'La "Réception" du B.E.M.', *Irénikon*, **59** (1986), pp. 32–59.

Locke, J. *On Toleration* (*Works*, London, 1801).

Lossky, V. *The Mystical Theology of the Eastern Church* (Cambridge: Clarke, 1957).

McGrath, A. E. 'The emergence of the Anglican tradition on justification', *Churchman*, **98** (1984), pp. 25–43.

McGrath, A. E. *Iustitia Dei* (Cambridge: CUP, 1986).

McGrath, A. E. *ARCIC II and Justification* (Oxford: Latimer House, 1987).

MacMurray, J. *Persons in Relation* (London: Faber, 1961).

McPartlan, P. 'Eucharistic ecclesiology', *One in Christ*, **22** (1986), pp. 314–31.

Mascall, E. L. *Christ, the Christian and the Church* (London: Longmans, 1946).

Maurice, F. D. *The Kingdom of Christ*, ed. A. R. Vidler (London: SCM, 1958).

Mersch, E. *The Whole Christ* (London: 1938).

Meyendorff, J. *Orthodoxy and Catholicity* (New York: Sheed & Ward, 1966).

Meyendorff, J. 'Unity of the Church — unity of mankind', *Ecumenical Review*, **24** (1972), pp. 30–46.

Meyendorff, J. *Byzantine Theology* (Oxford: Mowbray, 1975).

Meyer, H. 'The doctrine of justification in the Lutheran dialogue with other churches', *One in Christ*, **17** (1981), pp. 86–116.

Minnear, P. S. *Images of the Church in the New Testament* (London: Lutterworth Press, 1961).

Moltmann, J. *The Church in the Power of the Spirit* (London: SCM, 1977).

Moule, C. F. D. ' "Fulness" and "Fill" in the New Testament', *Scottish Journal of Theology*. **4** (1951), pp. 79–86.

Moule, C. F. D. *The Holy Spirit* (Oxford: Mowbray, 1978).

Newbigin, L. *The Household of God* (London: SCM, 1964).

Newman, J. H. *Lectures on Justification* (2nd edn; London, 1840).

Newman, J. H. 'Faith the title for justification', *Parochial Sermons*, vol. 6 (London, 1842).

Newman, J. H. *Apologia Pro Vita Sua* (London: Fontana, 1959).

Newsome, D. 'Justification and sanctification: Newman and the Evangelicals', *Journal of Theological Studies*, N.S. **15** (1964), pp. 32–53.

Palmer, W. *A Treatise on the Church of Christ* (2nd edn; London, 1839).

Patelos, G. (ed.) *The Orthodox Church in the Ecumenical Movement: Documents and Statements, 1902–1975* (Geneva: WCC, 1978).

Quick, O. C. *Doctrines of the Creed* (London: Nisbet, 1938).

Rahner, K. *Theological Investigations* (London: DLT, 1965–   ).

Ramsey, A. M. *The Gospel and the Catholic Church* (London: Longmans, 1936).

Ratzinger, J. *Church, Ecumenism and Politics* (Slough: St Paul, 1988).

Reardon, B. M. G. *From Coleridge to Gore* (London, 1971).

Richardson, A. *An Introduction to the Theology of the New Testament* (London: SCM, 1958).

Robinson, J. A. T. *The Body* (London: SCM, 1952).

Robinson, J. A. T. 'The One Baptism as a category of New Testament soteriology', *Scottish Journal of Theology*, **6** (1953), pp. 257–74; also in *Twelve New Testament Studies* (London: SCM, 1962).

Robinson, J. A. T. 'Kingdom, Church and Ministry' in K. M. Carey (ed.) *The Historic Episcopate* (Westminster: Dacre Press, 1954).

Rupp, E. G. *Studies in the Making of the English Protestant Tradition* (Cambridge: CUP, 1949).

Rupp, E. G. *Religion in England 1688–1791* (Oxford: Clarendon, 1986).

Santer, M. (ed.) *Their Lord and Ours* (London: SPCK, 1982).

Schaff, P. (ed.) *The Creeds of the Evangelical Protestant Churches* (London: Hodder & Stoughton, 1877).

Schillebeeckx, E. *Christ the Sacrament of Encounter with God* (London: Sheed & Ward, 1963).

Schleiermacher, F. D. E. *The Christian Faith* (Edinburgh: T. & T. Clark, 1928).

Schmemann, A. *Of Water and the Spirit* (New York: St Vladimir's Seminary Press, 1974).

Stillingfleet, E. *Irenicum* (2nd edn; London, 1662).

Stylianopoulos, T. 'The question of the reception of BEM in the Orthodox Church in the light of its ecumenical commitment', *Greek Orthodox Theological Review*, **30** (1985), pp. 205–28.

Sykes, S. W. and Booty, J. (eds) *The Study of Anglicanism* (London: SPCK; Philadelphia: Fortress, 1988).

Tappert, T. G. (ed.) *The Book of Concord* (Philadelphia: Fortress, 1959).

Taylor, J. *Liberty of Prophesying* (*Works*, London, 1839).

Taylor, J. V. *The Go-Between God* (London: SCM, 1971).

Thorndike, H. *Works* (LACT).

Thornton, L. *The Common Life in the Body of Christ* (3rd edn; London: Dacre, 1950).

Tillard, J.-M. R. 'The Church of God is a Communion: The ecclesiological perspective of Vatican II', *One in Christ*, **17** (1981), pp. 117–31.

Tillard, J.-M. R. 'Koinonia', *One in Christ*, **22** (1986), pp. 104–14.

Tillard, J.-M. R. *Église d'Églises* (Paris: Éditions du Cerf, 1987).

Tillard, J.-M. R. 'Canterbury and Rome: So near, so far', *One in Christ*, **25** (1989), pp. 139–52.

Torrance, T. F. *Royal Priesthood* (Edinburgh: Oliver & Boyd, 1955).

Torrance, T. F. *Conflict and Agreement in the Church* (London: Lutterworth, 1959).

Torrance, T. F. *Theology in Reconciliation* (London: Geoffrey Chapman, 1975).

Torrance, T. F. 'The goodness and dignity of man in the Christian tradition', *Modern Theology*, **4** (1988), pp. 309–22.

Trevelyan, G. M. *Clio: A Muse and Other Essays* (London, 1930)

Wake, W. *An Exposition of the Doctrine of the Church of England* (London, 1684).

Ware, K. (T.) *The Orthodox Church* (Harmondsworth: Penguin; 1963).

Ware, K. (T.) 'Church and eucharist: Communion and intercommunion', *Sobornost*, **7** (1978), pp. 550–68.

Waterland, D. *Of Fundamentals* (*Works*, Oxford, 1823).

Waterland, D. *A Summary View of the Doctrine of Justification* (*Works*, Oxford, 1823).

Willebrands, J. 'Vatican II's ecclesiology of Communion', *One in Christ*, **23** (1987), pp. 179–91.

Williams, R. 'Eastern Orthodox theology' in D. F. Ford (ed.) *The Modern Theologians II* (Oxford: Blackwell, 1989).

Wright, J. R. *Quadrilateral at One Hundred* (Cincinnati: Forward Movement; London: Mowbray, 1988).

Yarnold, E. *Can the Roman Catholic and Anglican Churches be Reconciled?* (London: SPCK/CTS, 1986).

Zizioulas, J. D. 'Some reflections on baptism, confirmation and eucharist', *Sobornost*, **5** (1969), pp. 644–52.

Zizioulas, J. D. *Being as Communion* (New York: St Vladimir's Seminary Press, 1985).

Zizioulas, J. D. 'The mystery of the Church in Orthodox tradition', *One in Christ*, **24** (1988), pp. 294–303.

Reports etc. in chronological order

Homilies appointed to be read in churches (London, 1864).

Doctrine in the Church of England (London: SPCK, 1938).

Church of Scotland, *Interim Report of the Special Commission on Baptism* (1955).

Anglican–Lutheran International Conversations (London: SPCK, 1973).

Ware, K. and Davey, C. (eds), *Anglican–Orthodox Dialogue: The Moscow Agreed Statement* (London: SPCK, 1977).

The Final Report of ARCIC I (London: SPCK/CTS, 1982).

'Justification by Faith' (Lutheran/Roman Catholic), *Origins*, **13** (1983), pp. 277–304.

Anglican–Orthodox Dialogue: The Dublin Agreed Statement 1984 (London: SPCK, 1984).

God's Reign and Our Unity (London: SPCK; Edinburgh: St Andrew, 1984).

Growth in Agreement (New York: Geneva, 1984).

Board of Mission and Unity, *The Priesthood of the Ordained Ministry* (London: Church House, 1986).

'Foi, Sacrements et Unité de l'Église', *Irénikon*, **61** (1987), pp. 336–49.

Salvation and the Church: An Agreed Statement by the Second ARCIC (London: Church House, 1987).

The Ordination of Women to the Priesthood: A Report by the House of Bishops (G.S. 764) (General Synod, London, 1987).

' "Salvation and the Church": Observations of the CDF', *One in Christ*, **24** (1988), pp. 377–87.

Eames, R., *Report of the Archbishop of Canterbury's Commission on Communion and Women in the Episcopate 1989* (London: Church House, 1989).

Index of names